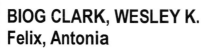

BIOG CLARK, WESLEY K.
Felix, Antonia

Wesley K. Clark.

4

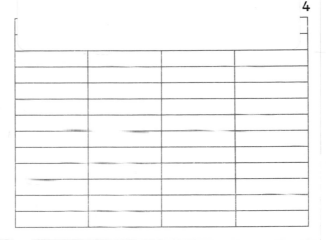

PLEASE
DO NOT REMOVE
CARD
FROM POCKET

WESLEY K. CLARK

A

BIOGRAPHY

★ ★ ★ ★

Other Newmarket Press titles by Antonia Felix

Condi: The Condoleezza Rice Story

WESLEY K. CLARK

A

BIOGRAPHY

★ ★ ★ ★

Antonia Felix

Newmarket Press • New York

*To the memory of James Gustaf Berg,
father, artist, and Navy man*

★ ★ ★ ★

This book is published in the United States of America.

First Edition

10 9 8 7 6 5 4 3 2 1

ISBN 1-55704-625-5

Library of Congress Cataloging-in-Publication Data

Felix, Antonia.
   Wesley K. Clark : a biography / Antonia Felix.—1st ed.
   p. cm.
Includes bibliographical references and index.
ISBN 1-55704-625-5 (hardcover : alk. paper)
1. Clark, Wesley K. 2. Generals—United States—Biography. 3. United States. Army—Biography. 4. Presidential candidates—United States—Biography. 5. North Atlantic Treaty Organization. 6. Kosovo (Serbia) —History—Civil War, 1998-1999. 7. Yugoslav War, 1991-1995. I. Title.

E840.5.C58F45 2004
973.931'092—dc22

2004007082

QUANTITY PURCHASES
Companies, professional groups, clubs, and other organizations may qualify for special terms when ordering quantities of this title. For information, write Special Sales Department, Newmarket Press, 18 East 48th Street, New York, NY 10017; call (212) 832-3575; fax (212) 832-3629; or e-mail mailbox@ newmarketpress.com.

www.newmarketpress.com

Manufactured in the United States of America.

CONTENTS

★ ★ ★ ★

"And may we not say confidently of man also, that he who is likely to be gentle to his friends and acquaintances, must by nature be a lover of wisdom and knowledge?"

"That we may safely affirm."

"Then he who is to be a really good and noble guardian of the State will require to unite in himself philosophy and spirit and swiftness and strength?"

"Undoubtedly."

"Then we have found the desired natures...."

—Plato, from *The Republic*

PREFACE

✯ ✯ ✯ ✯

On the morning of October 4, 1957, twelve-year-old Wesley Clark walked the three blocks to Pulaski Heights Junior High from home as usual. He was in the eighth grade, and in a couple of months he would be a teenager. After school, he did his homework at his desk in his room and later sat down to supper with his mother, stepfather, and his grandparents, who lived with them. It was a typical Friday evening in Little Rock, or so it seemed. They would learn the next day, however, that something new had come into the world that Friday, something that would fill households across the nation with fear and anxiety and chart a new course for the country. On Saturday, radio and newspaper reports spread the news: The Russians had launched a satellite in space that was circling the Earth once every ninety-six minutes. American ham radio operators had even confirmed it by picking up *Sputnik*'s odd bleeping signal. The nation's fear was matched by outrage; if the Russians controlled space, it was only a matter of time before they controlled the planet. How could they be technologically superior? How close were U.S. scientists to launching their own "artificial moon" into the sky?

Wesley was only twelve, but his instinct was to figure out how to be part of the solution. He had spent years playing soldier, setting up battles with his toy GIs and tanks in the backyard. But this event, along with other

Cold War realities, proved that the nation's new battles weren't going to be limited to military confrontations, like the war in Korea. The day after the launch, the Soviet Union boldly announced that "the new socialist society" had turned a glorious dream of mankind into reality.[1] America's most critical battle suddenly became a race for the mastery of space. It was a war of science, in which the victor would have the most brainpower and the resources to put that power into satellites and the rockets to launch them.

If science was the new frontier for defending the country, Wesley wanted to be part of it. He was excellent in math; it had always come easily to him. Now he had a tangible problem to work on, a challenge that took math out of the classroom and into the real world. As part of his self-styled introduction to rocket science, he bought his first rocket kit and put it together in his room. He went to the library to find books on rockets and delved into issues of science that were well beyond what he would he learn in high school. The rocket he built, along with many others that followed, actually worked; he launched them from his backyard. And there was another side to his strategy as well. "Know your enemy," he told himself, and he checked out a beginner's Russian textbook at a college library and began studying the language.

Clark's response to *Sputnik* is an early example of his self-motivation and his ability to find creative solutions to complex problems. Years later, as an army officer, nothing would satisfy him more than the opportunity to turn ideas into practical applications, whether in writing strategy or in helping propose high-tech military systems. And for thirty-four years it would always be about applying those ideas in the military, as a way to serve his country.

Sputnik ignited his desire to protect and serve, but other events during the Cold War contributed, too. A few years earlier, in 1951, Clark sat by the radio listening to Douglas MacArthur's farewell speech before Congress, in which the general intoned chilling facts about America's greatest enemy. *The Communist threat is a global one. Its successful advance in one sector threatens the destruction of every other sector. . . . Like a cobra, any new enemy will more likely strike whenever it feels that the. . . potential is in its favor on a worldwide basis.*[2] "My country was in danger, and I wanted to protect it," Clark later recalled.[3]

And in 1961, four years after *Sputnik*, Clark was about to enter his junior year of high school when President John F. Kennedy made his impassioned speech before Congress about America's future in space. To Clark and other young science and math whizzes, his words were like a sacred call:

> First, I believe that this nation should commit itself to achieving the goal, before this decade is out, of landing a man on the moon and returning him safely to the earth. No single space project in this period will be more impressive to mankind, or more important for the long-range exploration of space; and none will be so difficult or expensive to accomplish. . . . In a very real sense, it will not be one man going to the moon—if we make this judgment affirmatively, it will be an entire nation. For all of us must work to put him there.[4]

Kennedy's vision had a tremendous impact on Clark, as it did on many youth. By this time, he had become comfortable with thinking outside the box. For him, high school physics was more than an introduction to the nuts-and-bolts of how nature works; it was also an inspiration to think and imagine big. This curiosity and excitement about science has stayed with him throughout his life, and it came up during his campaign for the Democratic presidential nomination in 2003. At a small gathering, a former astronaut asked him about his plans for the space program, which led to a long, detailed answer about potential new breakthroughs in science, including traveling faster than light.

When this story was reported throughout the international press, the world was surprised to hear a recently retired four-star general wax on almost dreamily about the future of man in space. But it was quintessential Clark—visionary, creative, well-studied, and enthusiastic. It offered a glimpse of his complexity.

This book aspires to tell the personal and professional story behind that complexity. It is a family story that is unique in some ways, yet wholly American in that it traces the path of immigrants who had dreams for a better life in this country, and of a boy nurtured by the mantra that you can achieve anything if you work hard enough for it.

ONE

✯ ✯ ✯ ✯

Beyond the Pale

"The American dream has always depended on the dialogue between the present and the past."
—Robert A. M. Stern

The Festival of Lights was extra bright for the Kanne family of Chicago in 1944. On December 23rd, the posh Hyde Park area of the city's south side glowed with holiday lights strung in the trees and along the shop windows. At Michael Reese Hospital, an anxious Benjamin Kanne (pronounced KAY-nee) paced the hall until a nurse came through the door to announce that his wife had delivered a healthy baby boy. Kanne, a tall, handsome attorney who had made a name for himself in Chicago politics, was anxious to spread the good news. He and his wife, Veneta, would name the baby Wesley, after Veneta's grandfather, Thomas Wesley Reynolds. There was family to call—his brother, sisters, and Grandmother Ida. Benjamin's father had not lived long enough to see the birth of his boy; Jacob Kanne had died just two years before. That generation was almost gone, widening the gap between the old world and the new.

The untimely death of Benjamin Kanne himself nearly four years later would ultimately prevent Wesley Kanne Clark from learning this part of his family story until he was an adult in his twenties. It is a family legacy that stretches back to nineteenth-century Russia, where

Wesley's great-grandfather, Meyer Numerofsky, was born. Meyer began his journey to the New World in the late 1890s when he fled Belorussia with his grown family. Immigration records are inconsistent about which city they came from; some list Minsk and others state Pinsk, but either city made them residents of Belorussia. The exact date of their departure is unknown. "A lot of it's oral history," explained Wesley Clark's cousin Barry Kanne.[1]

Jews had been forced to move to Belorussia and near-by regions around the Black Sea during the reign of Catherine II. In 1835, Czar Nicholas I wrote a decree that defined the boundaries of the region, known as the Pale of Settlement. This ruling, which remained policy until 1917, placed all Russian Jews in a territory that was once part of the Polish kingdom, including present-day Lithuania, Belarus, Poland, Ukraine, Moldova, and other western parts of the Russian empire. The Pale of Settlement was one of the legal means by which the fiercely anti-Semitic empire kept Jews at a distance from the major cities of Russia. Jews were not allowed to farm, but made up the group of merchants, craftsmen, and shopkeepers that formed a separate class between the nobility and the peasants.

After Czar Alexander II was assassinated in 1881, Jews were blamed for his death and anti-Semitism flared up throughout the peasant population. The government did nothing to halt the riots, or pogroms, against the Jews that broke out in the Pale, and official propaganda even encouraged them. In 1881 alone, 200 pogroms occurred, in which approximately forty Jews were killed and hundreds of women raped. Pogrom violence ranged from arson and looting to rape and murder; in 1884, the most vicious pogrom broke out in Nizhniy Novgorod, where

Jews were hacked to death with axes and heaved from rooftops. An estimated 100,000 Jews were killed in the last wave of pogroms that struck the Pale between 1918 and 1921—in spite of Jewish self-defense units that had been developed over the years.

The Kanne family history, dating back to those times, is an immigration story traced from a dark period of history. The pogroms, coupled with the poverty that had devoured Belorussia for decades and a growing Zionist movement all ignited a mass emigration of Jews in the late nineteenth century. The Pale of Settlement, in which the majority of the world's Jews lived, contributed the largest numbers of Jewish immigrants to the United States in that period. Between 1880 and 1925, the Jewish population in the United States grew from 280,000 to approximately 4.5 million. Meyer Numerofsky, Wesley Clark's great-grandfather, was among those numbers. With his wife, Malka, and their grown children, Benjamin, Anna, Hortense, Fanny, Samuel, and Jacob, he made it safely to Switzerland. He purchased passports bearing the family name Kanne, and the group set off for the United States.[2]

The New World, as everyone had promised, was full of opportunity. The Kannes set up a dry goods and hardware store in Chicago called Kanne's Fair at 2806 South State Street. Jacob Kanne (Wesley's grandfather) married another Russian immigrant, Ida Goldman, in 1894, and they would have seven children over the next twelve years. But Meyer's son, Samuel, did not fare as well. He had married soon after arriving in Chicago, too, but there was a cloud hanging over him that the family lore has not been able to sort out. In the middle of the Chicago winter of 1907 he committed suicide. The death notice stated that he was found at the family store, where he had hung himself with a piece of cloth attached to a shelf. Death came, according to the death notice, "with suicidal intent while despondent." He was forty-one years old.[3]

Six months earlier, the Kannes had lost their patriarch, Meyer, in another dramatic fashion. On September 19, 1906, his body was found lying in the street at 14th and Canal. It was determined that he had dropped dead from a heart attack, or "chronic endocarditis."[4] At only sixty years old, his life in the New World was cut short and no one had expected it. Meyer's son Jacob died in Chicago in 1942, two-and-a-half years before the birth of his grandson, Wesley. Jacob's wife, Ida, survived him by thirteen years and is buried next to him at Waldheim Jewish Cemetery in Chicago.

Benjamin Kanne, Wesley's father, had graduated at the top of his class from the Chicago-Kent School of Law and was a member of the navy reserve. He served as an ensign during World War I but did not get assigned to a combat mission. Early in his career he became an assistant prosecutor in Chicago, and by the mid-1920s he was eager to get more involved in politics. He aimed for a seat on the city council; and in 1927 resigned from his position in the prosecutor's office to campaign for the office of alderman of the Fourth Ward, the area that includes the Hyde Park neighborhood. This move made the Chicago papers and solidified Kanne's reputation as a politically ambitious man to watch. The campaign increased his visibility among the constituents of the Fourth Ward, but he lost the election to Republican Berthold Cronson. Following this defeat, Kanne went back to work, this time as an attorney for the Chicago Sanitary District, a municipal corporation independent of the City of Chicago. The district controls the waterway for sewage in the Chicago area as well as the sewage treatment for the

city. Kanne's stature within the Democratic Party continued to grow throughout the Democratic administrations
of mayors William Dever, Anton Cermak, Frank Corr,
Edward Kelly, and Martin H. Kennelly.

Benjamin Kanne's role at the district came to an end
when he won a plum appointment in the city's legal system—assistant corporation counsel.[5] In this senior position, which he held for seventeen years, he was an attorney providing legal counsel and representation for the
city. In 1932 he was a delegate at the Democratic
National Convention, which was held in Chicago, and
nominated New York Governor Franklin Delano
Roosevelt for president. For three years he served as a
secretary for the Fourth Ward Democratic Organization,
and at one point worked alongside future mayor Richard
J. Daley, who would become Chicago's last "Big Boss."[6]
He also joined a private law firm with his younger brother, Louis E. Kanne, who had graduated from
Northwestern University and DePaul University's
College of Law.

Benjamin married a Methodist who had moved to
Chicago from Arkansas. Veneta Updegraff was a pretty
brunette with dark eyes and a charming accent, and she
had moved north to find better job opportunities. "She
was beautiful," said Wesley's second cousin Mary
Etzbach Campbell. "She was the most gorgeous person.
Dark hair, dark complexion, high cheekbones." Mary
remembered that she was taller than many of the other
mothers and that she walked with purpose. "For her time
she was not considered small; she was about 5'5" or 5'6"."[7]
Veneta's independent streak had brought her to Chicago,
just as it had driven her to get her own apartment in
Little Rock at age eighteen. There she had worked as a
stenographer for Republic Powers and Service Co. and

dated a young man named John Thomas Bogard Jr. They were married in 1926, but relatives said it was just "a teen-age thing" and the marriage only lasted about three years.[8]

Veneta was ambitious and restless. After her divorce, she packed her bags and moved to Chicago, where she got an apartment and landed a secretarial job. One day, as she struggled to unlock her door while carrying an armload of groceries, a dashing and courteous man— Benjamin Kanne—came to her rescue. His father owned the apartment building. From the start the attraction was mutual; they began dating, and in March 1939, got married in Niagara Falls, New York. Upon their return they settled into an upper-middle-class lifestyle in an apartment near Hyde Park. Veneta was in her thirties, and for the first time she didn't have to work.[9] She gave birth to Wesley when she was thirty-eight years old, and named him after her maternal grandfather.

Although Veneta had left a relatively large family back in Arkansas—both parents, two brothers, and a sister—she married into a large and close-knit Jewish clan. The entire extended family of brothers, sisters and cousins met up at least once a week. "They got together on weekends at the Kanne grandparents," said Wesley's cousin Barry Kanne, "and always had family meals there."[10] They met for Sabbath on Friday night and again on Sunday afternoon. After Jacob died, Grandmother Ida continued the tradition. It was all new for the daughter of a mill worker from Arkansas. The Hyde Park section of Chicago, south of downtown with a border on Lake Michigan and also incorporating the University of Chicago, was an affluent neighborhood that had been designed as a fashionable suburb in the mid-1800s. Benjamin Kanne fit into the intellectual aura of this neighborhood as an attorney for the city, an assistant prosecutor with a bright future, and a zealous loyalty to the local Democratic Party.

Mixed marriages such as Benjamin and Veneta's were not common at the time. Although Benjamin attended the KAM Isaiah Israel Temple, home of the oldest Jewish congregation in Chicago, and was proud of his family's heritage, he was not overtly religious. There was never a conflict over Veneta keeping her own faith and attending Sunday services at a Methodist church.[11] Veneta was disturbed by the discrimination that the Kannes and other Jews suffered in the city, and both she and Benjamin wanted to shield their son from that reality. "My mother told me once that she and my father agreed that I would not be brought up Jewish in Chicago," said Clark.[12] She also told him about the day-to-day realities that made them come to that decision. "She would reminisce a lot about it," he said. "There were restaurants they couldn't go to. There were clubs they couldn't belong to. There were resorts they couldn't go to vacation to. There were friends they didn't really have. This was a prejudiced society."[13] In addition, according to Jewish law, Wesley was not Jewish because the tradition is matrilineal; according to Judaic law, only those born to a Jewish mother are Jewish.

Veneta brought Wesley to the Methodist church on Sunday mornings rather than to his father's temple services on Saturday. Only decades later would Wesley learn about his Jewish ancestry and discover that his father and grandfather's gravestones carried the phrase, in Hebrew, "A descendant of the Kohen tribe." This phrase is the traditional way to indicate that the man—and his male descendants—descend from the Kohen rather than Levi and Yisrael tribes.

Wesley brought up his Kohen designation early in his 2004 bid for the Democratic presidential nomination, stating that he was from the priestly caste of Kohens.[14] Kohen (or Cohen, the Hebrew word for priest) is the lineage descended from Aaron, the brother of Moses, who was the first High Priest in Jewish history. For centuries, members of this caste lived by strict laws of purity and performed rituals in the temple. Some of the High Priests held enormous influence and power in politics and society that rivaled that of kings. To this day, the priestly stature of the Kohanim is evident in Orthodox and some conservative synagogues where only Kohanim are allowed to perform certain religious rites. A Kohan, for example, stands before the Ark of the Torah and recites the Priestly Blessing of the people. (The hand gesture of this blessing— fingers grouped in twos and split into a V—became part of American popular culture when actor Leonard Nimoy, who had seen it at the synagogue in his youth, used it as Spock's "Live long and prosper" sign in *Star Trek*.)

All descendants of Aaron are considered Kohanim— blood descendants of Aaron—and the status has been passed down by word of mouth from father to son throughout each generation. This makes them the oldest Jewish line that dates back 3,300 years, predating rabbis.[15] Many Kohanim are eager for proof beyond their oral family histories, and a study published in 1997 offered promise that a genetic test may be developed in the future. A research team compared the Y chromosomes of 68 Kohanim and 120 other Jewish men. They specifically looked at aspects of the chromosome that are passed from fathers to sons, as the Kohanim is a patrilineal line. The men who identified themselves as Kohanim all shared "certain distinctive genetic traits, indicating that they may represent a single line tracing back to one male forbear, perhaps even to Aaron."[16] The scientists' goal was to find physical evidence to support the lineage, not to develop a lab test that could prove it in individual men. But the news brought a strong response: "I have been inundated with requests for testing," said one of the scientists who ran the experiment.[17]

Even though Wesley's father was part of a Reformed congregation, which does not adhere to many of the laws of Orthodox Judaism, the marking on his tombstone reveals that he was proud to be part of this lineage. Another indication of the Kanne family's identification with the Kohanim is the name their patriarch chose when he obtained his passport in Switzerland. Kohen surnames include Cohen, Kohn, Kone, Kahn, Kagan, Kogen, and Kahane. When Wesley's great-grandfather dropped the name Numerofsky, he chose Kanne—perhaps because it echoed other Kohen derivatives.

Wesley Clark remembers his father as a doting, loving parent who played with him, read to him every night, and bought him gifts every week. "He was a big factor in my life," he said. "I remember he went out to buy me a present every Saturday. . . . He loved three things: pinochle, horses, and politics—plus my mother and me."[18] Wesley also recalled that his father loved baseball and cigars, and that he let him sit on his lap in the car when they drove around on the weekends. "On Saturdays, we would go out, sometimes to a museum, or shopping," said Wesley. "It was our day."[19] He basked in the attention until the night his father died, just seventeen days before Wesley's fourth birthday. "My father was a tremendous influence in my life," Clark said, "and then one night he read to me, and I woke up in the middle of the night and there were a lot of adults in the apartment. They kept me from going in the bedroom, and that was the night he died."[20]

Benjamin's death was a shock to everyone. That day, he had gone to the doctor for a routine checkup and left with a clean bill of health. He was fifty-two years old and in the prime of his life. But that night, on December 6, 1948, his heart failed and he died in his sleep. The shock traumatized Wesley so much that he developed a speech impediment that he would grapple with for years.

Benjamin Kanne's funeral was held at a chapel on East 47th Street in Chicago, and the crowd who attended revealed what a major figure he was. "The constituents were lined up for blocks to pay their respects to Wesley's father," said Wesley's cousin Harriet Salk.[21]

Even though Wesley only knew his father for the first four years of his life, he realizes that the love and attention that the man showered on him created a solid foundation of emotional well being. "I think that the warmth that you give a child when they are very young is something that they carry throughout their entire life," Clark said, "and he was very warm and he was very charismatic. He was a politician. He was a people person. He was the star of his family."[22]

A profile of Clark in the *Boston Globe* stated that Benjamin Kanne left very little for his wife and son to live on. "He left behind a diamond ring . . . and, according to probate records, a four-door Buick worth $250, and $464.68 after funeral and court costs."[23] (Years later, Clark's wife had the diamond from Kanne's ring set in Clark's West Point ring as a surprise thirtieth birthday present.) Although Benjamin made a good living, "he spent it as quickly as he made it," according to one family member.[24] Veneta was too saddened by the memories of her husband to stay in Chicago. She decided it would be best to return to Arkansas; Little Rock would be less expensive than Chicago, and her large family and familiar surroundings would provide emotional support to get through her loss. She knew that she would have to find full-time work, and in Little Rock she had two brothers, a sister, and her parents to help take care of Wesley while she worked.

Perhaps the most compelling reason for Veneta's move back to Little Rock was the fact that she did not feel particularly close to the Kanne family. "My sense, from comments over the years, is that Veneta was not a welcome addition to the family and when Ben died, she probably felt alone in Chicago," said Clark's cousin Barry Kanne. He conjectured that because Veneta was not Jewish, the family never considered her an insider. She was in an awkward position; even though her husband had had no qualms about marrying outside the religion, it was a nontraditional thing to do, especially at that time. Veneta was not shunned by the family, but she was never really brought into the fold either. "She was probably a pretty lonely person in Chicago," said Barry. Benjamin did not object to raising Wesley as a Christian, but in general, the Kannes would have preferred that he had married a Jewish woman and raised a Jewish family. It was not so much a matter of Wesley's religious upbringing, but a matter of ancestry and tradition. "None of us were raised in a particularly devout way," explained Kanne. "We were Jewish by birth and we observed many of the holidays and traditions, but I certainly would not characterize us as a strongly religious family."[25]

After the move to Little Rock, Veneta made certain that Wesley would not know anything about his Jewish ancestry. He kept his name until the fifth grade, when

Veneta remarried—at that point his middle name was changed from Jay to Kanne—but he did not learn anything about the ancestry behind that name. Veneta kept in touch with the Kannes through letters to and from Florence Ellis, one of Benjamin's sisters, but she kept this correspondence private. Chicago's prejudicial treatment of Jews had been an eye-opening experience, and when Veneta returned to Little Rock she realized there was a history of discrimination against Jews in the South as well. Before she married Benjamin Kanne, she had not had much reason to think about it. But now she was determined to protect her son from the anti-Semitism in the South.

Little Rock had a separate country club for Jews, just like Chicago. And most southern Jews kept low-key about their heritage in an attempt to blend in, as Jack Nelson explains in his book about the Ku Klux Klan and anti-Semitism, *Terror in the Night*:

> Even when they tried to convince themselves of their acceptance by their fellow Southerners, deep down they always knew they were viewed as aliens in a land of un-compromising, militant, fundamentalist Protestantism. . . . To thrive, many Jews concluded, they had to assimilate into the dominant culture in every way possible. Becoming "200 percent Southerners," they submerged their own religious and cultural heritage . . . partly out of fear of the violence that never seemed far below the surface in Mississippi.[26]

The Klan had been publishing anti-Semitic propaganda since World War I, when the issue of Jews in the armed forces was debated throughout the country. Hiram Evans, Imperial Wizard of the Klan from 1922 to 1939,

remarked on the "Jewish problem" that Jews were inas-
similable "with no deep national attachment, a stranger
to the emotion of patriotism as the Anglo-Saxon feels
it."[27] By the time Wesley had left Arkansas to go to West
Point and Oxford, anti-Semitism in the Klan had heated
up to new levels with Mississippi Klansman Sam Bower's
idea that the Jews were at the heart of an international
Communist conspiracy. Bower launched a new, more violent faction of the Klan in order to fight against the Jews
and blacks in the civil rights movement. To Bower, the
movement was a concoction of the Jews to "mongrelize"
the nation and destroy white Christian society.[28] In 1964,
civil rights workers Michael Schwerner, James Chaney,
and Andrew Goodman were shot by Klansmen and
buried beneath an earthen dam in Mississippi. Three
years later, the Klan bombed a synagogue in Jackson,
Mississippi, as well as the home of the temple's rabbi.

Fundamentalist Bible Belt Christianity was another
source of anti-Semitic overtones in the South. The evangelical movement—which believes in a literal translation
of the Bible and in Jesus as the only hope for "personal
salvation"—exploded from the rural South in the 1960s.
In this belief system, Jews are not only doomed because
of their lack of a personal relationship with Jesus, they
are guilty of deicide according to the New Testament.[29]
Reverend Bailey Smith, former president of the
Southern Baptist Convention, made national news when
he unabashedly stated that God does not hear the
prayers of Jews. Although not all Baptists hold these rad-
ical evangelical beliefs, of course, the growing numbers
of evangelicals in the South contributed to anti-Jewish
sentiment.

In 1949, Veneta and Wesley moved into her parents'

apartment at 14th and Cumberland in downtown Little Rock, about two blocks west of MacArthur Park. Robert and Nora "Elsie" Updegraff had been married for forty-five years, and Robert was a retired lumber mill worker. He had moved his family around to several Arkansas mill towns such as Dumas, Pine Bluff, and Dierks where he got jobs sawing trees into boards. He also worked at a lumber company in Little Rock for a time. His father had been a farmer in Oklahoma, and the first Updegraffs had come from Germany and settled in Pennsylvania. Robert was a quiet and kind man who loved to tell stories to the kids who came around the house.

Wesley's maternal grandmother, Elsie Reynolds Updegraff, came from Irish and English immigrants. She was born in Carrollton, in northwest Arkansas, to Thomas Wesley Reynolds, a carpenter, and Mary "Emma" Upshaw. Emma's father (Wesley's great-great grandfather), H. H. Upshaw, was a doctor from Carrollton who was as in demand for his fine fiddle-playing as he was for his skill at delivering babies. An advertisement in the *Carroll County Bowlder* from 1877 described his medical services:

H. H. UPSHAW
Physician, Surgeon and Accoucheur,
Carrollton, Arkansas.

Returns thanks for past patronage, and hopes to merit a continuance of the same by prompt attention to business. Special attention given to Chronic Diseases of Females.[30]

"Accoucheur" was a term in those days for a male midwife or obstetrician. Part of the Upshaw family history that is still not verified is the identity of H. H. Upshaw's mother. His father had married twice, and records indicate that one of his wives may have been a woman who married a man named Ezekiel Starr, who was one-quarter Cherokee. "There's a story that the Indians came and took H. H. one time and brought him back later on," said Wesley's second cousin Mary Campbell. "The story was he was part Indian; I think they probably just had someone in the tribe who was sick and they needed a doctor."[31]

Elsie Updegraff, Wesley's grandmother who lived with him and his mother, was a product of the Reynolds-Upshaw line and, in the words of Campbell, "a typical southern lady. She was the protective type, and you also had to toe the mark with her." Mary, who is four years older than Wesley and was one of his playmates, said her father was the same way. "Wesley and all of us kids learned to respect our elders," she said. "When talking to my father, if you failed to say 'Yes, sir' or 'No, sir,' he would stop you with, 'What did I hear you say?' He was known as a hard-headed Dutchman."

Mary Campbell's mother, Daisy, and Veneta were first cousins, nearly the same age and very close—"like sisters," according to Mary. Wesley was inundated with the philosophy that a person can do anything he sets his mind to, and Mary saw this attitude at work in his life, even as a young child. "Whatever he wanted to do, he set his mind to accomplish it," she said. "The thought never crossed his mind that he couldn't do anything. We were both brought up that way. My dad and everyone in this family would say, 'there's no such word as can't.'"[32] Veneta tried to teach Wesley by example that hard work pays off. Wesley was her jewel, she "protected and bragged on him" and was backed up by her own parents who were just as protective and just as proud.[33]

The trajectory of Wesley's life at his birth may have aimed at a future in the law or in Chicago politics, to trace a career in his father's footsteps. But that trajectory took a turn after his father's death. Surrounded by a new family in Little Rock, Wesley had a sort of second birth between the ages of four and five. From that point on he would be brought up as a southerner, his mother would eventually remarry, and he would be taught by his stepfather to fish and hunt and enjoy the Arkansas wilderness. He would uncover an abiding interest in religion, nurtured by the Baptist church, and rise to the top in academics as well as in his chosen sport. He would also become immersed in a sense of civic responsibility and service to country that pervaded the boys' organizations he joined in Little Rock.

★ ★ ★ ★

"Boy of the Year"

> "Youth is a time when we find the
> books we give up but do not get over."
> —Lionel Trilling[1]

Shortly after moving to Little Rock in 1949, Veneta asked Wesley which church he wanted to go to. He was only four-and-a-half years old, but she told him that it was his choice. Chicago was still vivid in his mind, and he made his decision based on something he had loved about the church he had attended there with his mother. "I remember the Methodist church in Chicago had these beautiful stained-glass windows," he said. "So I saw a church in Arkansas that had those beautiful stained-glass windows . . . [and] I picked that church."[2] His choice, Immanuel Baptist on 10th and Bishop Streets, was about thirty blocks west of his grandparents' apartment where they were living. Even though he would soon move to another part of town, he kept going to Immanuel, showing up on Sunday mornings in a little suit.

Clark's independent attitude about going to church on his own was typical of how he made his way in Little Rock. From that young age, as an only child without a father, he learned to venture out on his own to build his own interests and forge his own path in life. "I discovered when I went down to Arkansas as a kid that when you don't have a father, you sort of got to make your own way in life. It's really up to you," Clark said. "There's really nobody there.

You've got to do it. I didn't have a big brother or anybody to sort of take care of me," he said. "I took care of myself."[3]

By the time Wesley was ready to start school in 1950, Veneta had worked long enough as a secretary at Commercial Bank to afford to buy a house in Pulaski Heights, one of Little Rock's nicest neighborhoods west of downtown. The house, at 506 North Valentine Street, was a one-story with a red brick foundation and screened-in front porch. The Heights was the perfect location for raising a child, with Pulaski Heights Elementary and Junior High just around the corner on Lee Avenue. Allsop Park, a mini-forest with ballparks, was just five blocks away. Wesley's grandparents moved in with them, so there was always someone around while Veneta was working during the day. Pulaski Heights was home to an affluent middle-class of bank presidents, auto-dealership owners, and jewelry-store merchants, and Wesley recalled that he was "the poorest kid in the richest neighborhood" in Little Rock.[4]

Veneta was in her mid-forties when Wesley started school, still very much the attractive woman that had won the heart of Benjamin Kanne. A few years after moving back to Little Rock she got serious about another man, Victor Clark, whom she met in the city's banking community. The family is not certain whether Victor was working with Veneta at Commercial Bank or if he worked for another bank at the time they met, but in any case their banking connection brought them together. They were married on November 20, 1954, when Veneta's son was in the fifth grade.

Victor was born in Berryville, Arkansas, not far from Carrollton where Veneta's mother was raised. His father, Baker Clark, was a teacher and a 33rd-degree Mason who traveled throughout Arkansas giving speeches about the Masonic Order. Victor's mother, Jeanette "Nettie" Clark, was a small but strong woman who, according to Wesley's cousin Terence B. Clark, "was called 'Big Grandmother' because of her power in the family." Nettie canned, gardened, and loved to fish. According to Terence, on a fishing day she would get up at 2:00 a.m. to fix fried chicken and chicken fried steak for an early breakfast before they all left together at 4:00 a.m., not to return until dusk. "Grandmother hated to be in the house," said Terence.[5]

Victor had been married for many years and divorced by the time he met Veneta. He and his first wife, Mary Williams, had one son, Kennard, who described his father as "outgoing, very masculine, a handsome man."[6] A tall, quiet, athletic type who had played semiprofessional basketball, Victor was close to his sister, Jewel, and he loved to take his family to the country home she shared with her husband, Alonzo "Lon" Dodson, in Paron, Arkansas. At this two-story log home in the woods about 32 miles west of Little Rock, Victor taught Kennard, and later Wesley, how to fish and shoot a gun.

Wesley's uncle Lon and aunt Jewel Dodson raised free-range hogs, chickens, and milk cows, and tended a large garden that nearly made them self-sufficient on their large acreage. Lon was a World War I veteran who went to Canada at age fifteen to enlist with the Canadian troops. He lied about his age and fought in the kilt-wearing Scottish regiment that the German's dubbed the "Ladies from Hell." After getting shot, he returned to Arkansas and, when the United States entered the war, enlisted in the Army and returned to combat. He was wounded again, this time in the pelvis, which prevented him from having children. "Grandmother Nettie was devastated when he married Jewel," said Terence Clark. "Jewel, she was the belle of Little Rock, and Nettie had great expectations for her and her future children." [7]

In 1949—the same year that Veneta and Wesley were on their way from Chicago to Arkansas—Victor had moved with his first wife and son to Dallas to take a job as a vice president at the First National Bank. It was an upward move from his job as an officer at the Federal Reserve Bank in Little Rock, where he had worked for twenty years. Kennard, who was seventeen when they moved to Dallas, recalled that his parents began to have problems at that time. "I knew they weren't getting along, but now my dad wanted a divorce. I remember trying to talk him out of it. He had his mind made up, and there wasn't any more to say. I never did talk to him after that."[8] Kennard attributed his reluctance to get in touch with his father as "sheer cussedness" because he felt his father should call him first. Part of Victor's marital problems stemmed from his struggle with alcohol, according to the family.[9] He attended Kennard's high school graduation in 1950, but divorced Mary and left Texas after that.[10]

Returning to his parents' farm, Victor told his family that he needed help tackling his alcoholism. "He came up to Berryville and realized he was in bad shape," said Terence Clark. "His mother paid for him to go to a rehab center." Terence's father drove Victor up to a facility in Kansas City, where Victor was successfully treated in about two months. He returned to Berryville to live with his parents and build up his strength by helping clear some of the fields. "He did a lot of physical work," said Terence, clearing trees and rocks for about three months. He did a good job of cleaning himself up."[11]

Victor looked for work in Little Rock and began putting his life back together. Veneta Kanne became a central point of that new life, and on November 20, 1954, they got married in Greenville, Mississippi, just over the border from Arkansas. There was no waiting period to get a marriage license in that state, and it was not unusual for Arkansas couples to make the one-stop outing to get a marriage license at the Washington County Courthouse and perform the ceremony the same day. Victor adopted Wesley Kanne, who at nine years old was renamed Wesley Clark, and within a short time everyone who knew Wesley assumed Victor had always been his father. None of his school friends knew about Wesley's birth in Chicago or about Benjamin Kanne. The adoption became official when Wesley turned sixteen and, according to custom, Wesley's birth certificate in Chicago was changed to reflect Victor Clark as his biological father. Later, Wesley would comment that he didn't think the revision was the right thing to do. "They shouldn't have done it," he said.[12] Wesley loved his stepfather, but he thought the act of erasing his father's name from his birth certificate was unnecessary.

Clark recalled that his stepfather had had a difficult time finding regular work and that Veneta was the sole wage earner during several periods of their lives. "The problem was that he'd gone through a very difficult divorce, he'd had too much to drink during the process, he had lost his reputation in the banking community," said Clark. "It was stressful on all of us. My mother loved him. My mother loved me. He tried to take care of us. She was the breadwinner, he was struggling. It was painful."[13] Clark was close to his stepfather, but always aware that his earlier marriage and circumstances had taken their toll. "I loved him dearly, but he hardly ever made any money because he'd been divorced and was an alcoholic. And he just had a hard time getting a job that was commensurate, really, with his ability."[14]

Victor talked to Wesley about his son, Kennard; how he taught him to fish, how Kennard had studied the piano, how they took vacations at the country house with Aunt Jewel and Uncle Lon. These conversations were sometimes awkward for Wesley, who could not help thinking about the boy who had lost the father he was now fortunate to have. Listening to "Kennard did this" and "Kennard did that" time and again was, in Wesley's words, "strange."[15] He did not learn the whereabouts of his stepbrother until an *Arkansas Democrat-Gazette* reporter wrote about the connection during the Democratic presidential nomination campaign in 2003. After the story came out, Wesley phoned Kennard, a surgeon in Arlington, Texas, and they talked about Victor Clark. He told the press he had heard about his father's death from a relative, but he did not know about Wesley until the reporter called him in 2003. The Clark family found this odd, in that Kennard's mother kept in very close touch with Wesley's Aunt Jewel and other members of the Clark family, and she knew everything about Wesley.

Wesley's neighborhood in Pulaski Heights was full of kids when he was growing up. The streets were for riding bikes and playing scrub—a type of baseball with rotating players instead of teams—the backyards were for building forts out of old Christmas trees, and the curb was for playing gossip—whispering a message down the line to hear how distorted it would get by the end. "It was a really great neighborhood," Wesley said. "We played sports every afternoon in the street after school, baseball during baseball season, football, basketball. We went up to Allsop Park a lot."[17]

Wally Loveless, who lived across the street from the Clarks, remembered groups of boys playing "Best Faller" and "Best Die-er," seeing who could collapse with the most flair and pretend to die with the best sound effects.

Another variation, when those got old, was "Funniest Faller." Even though Wally was younger, he spent a lot of time with Wesley because they lived so close and, as an only child, Wesley didn't mind the company. Wally and Wesley had swordfights—inspired by Prince Valiant comic strips—using garbage can lids for shields and blades that Wesley made out of fence slats. But more than anything else, the boys played soldiers in the back-yard. "There was a lot of military-type play in the neigh-borhood," Wally said. "Wesley had a bunch of army men and air force men and he'd set up battles in his shrubbery in the yard. Then he'd have the battle and throw the dirt up with the guys and have explosions." They made forts for the soldiers out of Lincoln Logs and built model planes to fly over their grassy battlefields.

Wesley was a prolific model builder, with model air-planes hanging from the ceiling of his bedroom and bat-tleships and PT boats on his shelves. Wally was thrilled when Wesley took him to the Hillcrest Variety store one day to pick out a model airplane kit. "For an older kid to want to go down to the store with you and help you was flattering," Wally recalled. He had his eye on a B52, but Wesley convinced him to buy a Japanese Zero. It didn't take long for Wally to figure out that Wesley needed an enemy plane to target during their backyard dogfights. "We could never shoot down the American planes because that would be unpatriotic," said Wally.[18]

Inside, the boys played board games and chess— Wally's father was a member of a chess-by-mail club and taught them to play. Wally spent hours over at the Clarks reading Wesley's huge collection of comic books. He had the usual superhero titles, such as *Spiderman* and *Superman*, but most of his comics were about America's fighting forces. *Combat, Battle Fire, Army War Heroes, GI*

Combat, and *Fightin' Army* were popular in the 1950s. Wally said that all the boys learned their gun sounds— *Budda, budda, budda* and *Ka-pow*—from comic books like these, and used them in their neighborhood army battles. Dressed in old helmet liners and uniform belts dangling with canteens and other accoutrements they bought at army surplus stores, the boys shot at invisible enemies with toy guns. They rarely divided into teams because no one wanted to play the enemy.

Only one house in the neighborhood had a television set that Wally and Wesley knew of. "Six or eight of us would go over to the Cogbills and watch TV in the dining room," said Wally. "Mr. Cogbill sold television sets in his jewelry store." He remembered the cartoon *Crusader Rabbit* and a popular interactive show, *Winky Dink,* which involved putting a plastic sheet over the screen and connecting the dots with the characters.[19]

Wesley spent time with girls, too, especially his older cousin, Mary Campbell. When she was about to leave the house, her mother would ask her to call Wesley and see if he wanted to tag along. "I used to take him to this theater on Saturday afternoons," she said. "He liked science fiction. One that I particularly remember was called *The Thing,* and it scared him to death. He squeezed my hand like everything."[20] Mary taught her little cousin how to ride a bike and took him to the city pool to swim and get sunburned. He also played with his cousin Cathy Hardy, who lived in the neighborhood, and Patty Loveless, Wally's sister, who was his age. Another girl who knew Clark growing up is the actress Mary Steenburgen, whose mother, Nell, worked with Veneta at the bank. The two women were best friends, and Mary recalled that Veneta often bragged about her son to Nell. Steenburgen and Clark's paths would cross again later in their lives.[21]

Patty Loveless came into the picture when Victor Clark was dating Veneta. Victor's courting included taking Veneta, Wesley, and the girl-next-door (actually, across the street) on picnics at Boyle Park. Patty and Wesley played in Rock Creek, which ran the length of park, building rock dams and wading in the water while Veneta and Victor picnicked on the grass. The two neighbors were friends all through their school years and graduated together in 1962. In those first years they often walked to Pulaski Heights Elementary together, and the school was so close that they also had time to walk home for lunch.[22]

Wesley's elementary teachers were tough and demanding. "The teachers were good and very strict," he said. "Our first-grade teacher was Mrs. Talbot. If you just barely got it, she'd say, 'You've made it by the skin of your teeth.' I remember coming home and saying to my grandmother, 'What does she mean by skin of my teeth?'" He gives the Pulaski Heights teachers credit for motivating him to do his best in those formative years. "These were great teachers," he said. "They taught you to apply yourself and that anything was possible if you cared enough. They made learning fun, but they also gave you a tremendous desire to excel."[23]

He received double doses of this motivational support with exacting teachers and a family with a can-do attitude. His mother was serious about everything pertaining to Wesley, from his education to his appearance. "She was a very strong woman," said Wesley. "She had strong ideas, and she was very protective of me. . . . She made sure I had a good school to go to. She drove me around. She worried about my clothing—things a mother would do."[24] Veneta was the driving force in Wesley's life, not his stepfather. Although Victor was kind, caring, and interested in all of Wesley's activities, it was Veneta who took action. "It was my mother who was pushing me," Wesley said.[25]

Wesley was serious about school, curious about everything, and self-motivated. His cousin Cathy Hardy said that they would play together after elementary school until Wesley decided it was time to do his homework. "Wes never had to be prodded," she said. "He would go in and sit at the mahogany desk and take care of business."[26] His academic excellence—which would eventually take him to two of the best colleges in the world—started early, and he attributed it to simple, unwavering curiosity. He was also serious about church, but his parents didn't share his interest and he usually attended by himself. When he was in the first grade, Wesley started going to Immanuel Baptist Church several times a week. He attended Sunday school as well as Bible readings on weekdays. After a couple of years, Veneta got tired of driving all the way to Immanuel and they had Wesley choose another church closer to home. He started attending Pulaski Heights Baptist Church on Kavanaugh Boulevard, about four blocks away from his house. Church had become an important part of his life, and it pained him that his parents didn't go. "I was always nagging my parents to come," said Wesley. "I think my mother and stepfather came once or twice. That was it. Other kids had their parents there."[27]

A very popular place in Little Rock for boys was the Boys' Club, housed in a large brick building on West Fifth Street. The club was established in 1917 to promote the healthy development of boys—physically, intellectually and socially—and to instill a sense of citizenship and leadership. In segregated Little Rock, the club was only open to whites; a separate facility was set up for blacks on the south side of town at 33rd and State.[28] (Also typical of the time, girls were not admitted until 1971.) Wesley's first involvement with the club was to take classes to overcome his speech impediment, which he did by age seven.

The Boys' Club would be a central part of Wesley's life, both athletically and socially, until he graduated from high school. When he was eleven years old, his stepfather had a heart-to-heart talk with him about competitive sports. Kindly but to the point, Victor said, "Kid, you're not going to be a basketball player."[29] Wesley had a small build for football and wasn't tall enough to make it in junior high basketball, which was coming up the next year. But he was ambitious and competitive and wanted to find a sport. He found it at the Boys' Club; in the eighth grade he joined the club's swimming team, coached by a man who would loom large in his life, Jimmy Miller. Wesley made a big impression on Miller, the club's athletic director, from the first day they met. He went home that night and told his wife, Boonie, about the new swimmer on his team.

"Honey, I've met the neatest young man and he's really going to go places."

"Who is it?" Boonie asked.

"Wesley Clark."

"What impressed you about him?"

"He's so clean-cut and ambitious, and he really listens to instructions. He wants to do everything right."[30]

It was the start of a discipline that Wesley kept up every day of his school and military careers and beyond, to the extent that some friends today call him "General Speedo."[31] From the start, Jimmy Miller watched as Wesley became a stellar competitor, loading up trophies and inspiring his teammates. Miller, who sported the same flattop haircut he had worn in the army in World War II, snapped towels at kids who got out of line and ran the athletic program like a command. His son, Chuck

Miller, described his father's way as "tough love," and added that everybody loved him for it. "He was a very strong disciplinarian from the standpoint of holding kids accountable," he said. "He was a sergeant in the army air force and flew in B19s, but he rarely talked about those days. The only story he ever told was how he got left on an island and all he had left was sardines and beer. The next morning the coral snakes were all over and they had to shoot them before they got out of the tent. He was a tail gunner in the Pacific theater. He told me he bombed haystacks where the Japanese hid munitions."[32]

The Millers were a large family with six children, and on any given night they would have up to another eight children camping out at the house. Their swimming pool also attracted hordes, all of whom were welcome. "We'd have 150 kids come to our own pool on an afternoon," said Chuck. "It was a real fun time for kids, with a lot of camaraderie. In Wesley's day, there wasn't a lot for kids to do, a pool was a gathering place. The Boys' Club and the YMCA in Little Rock were really the only venues for kids to get out. And of course parents dropped them off, and you've got to have someone who's going to watch them and discipline them."[33]

Wesley's commitment to swimming made the Boys' Club almost a second home. "The Boys' Club was a very important part of Wes's life," said Phillip McMath, a longtime friend and Little Rock native. "Jimmy Miller was a kind of father figure to him; he was very important in Wesley's life. Coach Miller was kind of your Irish uncle, everybody loved him, he had a lot of influence on boys. He was a fabulous swimming coach and he was completely selfless in his dedication to the kids."[34] Clark recalled that the club's director, Billy Mitchell, was also a big figure in their lives. "He was a tremendous athlete, but by this time he was seventy years old," he said. "He was a grandfather of all of us.... He was a really great guy. When it was time to get the letter to the principal to say you should be excused to go to a swim meet, Mr. Mitchell could always do that for you."[35]

In the spring of 1958, when Wesley was about to finish his last year at Pulaski Heights Junior High, he tried out for a job as camp counselor at the Joseph Pfeifer Kiwanis Camp, commonly known as the Boys' Club camp. Jimmy Miller ran the summer camp, which was about 20 miles west of Little Rock off State Highway 10. As Wesley reminisced in his book *Waging Modern War,* Miller took the counseling positions very seriously and spent months holding Saturday morning "leadership classes" for potential candidates. An inscription in the stonework above the Boys' Club doorway read, "ENTER YOU MEN OF TOMORROW," which reflected the club's commitment to shaping responsible citizens and leaders. No one took that job more seriously than Miller.

In April, the group of would-be counselors spent a weekend at the camp to help prepare for the arrival of campers in June. Wesley recounted that weekend as one of the most important in his childhood, when he learned the life lesson that "you have to have courage to attain your goals."[36] For him, that courage came in the form of jumping off a 42-foot-high bridge into Little Maumelle Creek on the orders of Miller. Early that Sunday morning, the boys walked down to the creek to skinny-dip, catch frogs, and play with their electric model boats. The coach spotted them as he drove over the old rusty iron bridge. He stopped and asked them what they were doing, and the rest of the conversation "remains in some dispute," according to Clark.[37]

He drove off but came back a few minutes later, chastising the boys for not returning to camp immediately as he had asked. As a result, they would have to pay for their misconduct by jumping off the bridge. Those who jumped would be counselors in June, those who didn't could only attend as campers. Six of the boys walked back to camp and four, including Wesley, stayed behind and began climbing up the iron girders to the top of the bridge. They had heard rumors about Miller and some other adults—the legendary Red Bridge Club—who allegedly did flips and dives off the bridge at night. The four boys stood on the narrow metal girder, naked, trying to talk the coach out of it. But Miller insisted that they would be fine if they just did a standing broad jump and aimed for the deep green-colored area that was a pool about six or seven feet deep. It sounded easy, but the boys knew that the rest of the creek was much more shallow. The anxiety reached a peak when they heard a vehicle coming down the road. A pickup with three women in the front seat appeared, and out of embarrassment, the oldest boy jumped. To his surprise, Wesley followed him after Miller counted, "One, two, three!"

At that moment, Wesley became a counselor and a bona fide member of the Red Bridge Club. "The afterglow lasted a good two weeks, at least," he wrote. "Or maybe forty years. You have to have courage and faith. And you have to expect to go through some trials to be a leader."[38]

As a counselor at the camp, Wesley was responsible for the sixteen boys in his cabin. Days began with a flag ceremony out on the lawn, where everyone stood in a semicircle and recited the Pledge of Allegiance. There were swimming lessons and nature hikes to learn about the local flora and fauna. The boys marched in formation, rotated for chores such as KP and latrine duty, recited prayers, played softball and horseshoes, and walked in file to the mess hall, a rustic wooden building with pane-less, open-air windows. Awards were given out for many activities, including Best Recitation of the Camp Creed and Best Prayer. Wesley proved to be a natural leader, as many of his friends would describe him later in high school. He enjoyed the responsibility and discovered the concept of public service. "Looking after the sixteen campers in the cabin gave me a keen sense of satisfaction," he wrote. "I had to get to know each one, learn his dispositions, strengths, and weaknesses, and help him to participate and achieve in the . . . programs."[39]

Miller made sure that the counselors understood the underlying purpose of all the sports, drills, nature lessons, and rules, a purpose written into the Camp Creed. The tenets of the ten-point creed were developed to shape the "Men of Tomorrow" as honest, loyal, service-oriented members of society, and included phrases such as "My body is a sacred temple which must be kept clean and strong"; "It is more honorable to lose than to win unfairly"; "It is best to act reverently in all matters relating to religion, womanhood, age, law, and tradition"; "I must be honest in every word, thought, and deed"; and "It is best to act with tolerance towards those whose thoughts or acts honestly differ from my own."[40] Wesley and the other counselors had learned the creed during their leadership courses in the spring and recited it at camp every day; each point became as familiar to them as the Pledge of Allegiance and the Lord's Prayer.

The lessons in character and honesty that Clark learned at the Boys' Club—as well as in his church and from his teachers—appeared to sink in, according to one story from his teenage years. In an episode that could be called his "George Washington and the Cherry Tree" story, Clark was riding around town with his friend Jerry

Bona and another friend one winter evening. The third boy made a dare to steal a red holiday bulb and put it on the front-porch light display at Jerry's girlfriend's house. Clark took a bulb from a string of lights on a grocery storefront, but just as they were about to drive away he insisted they wait for him. He wanted to slip a quarter beneath the door to pay for the light. "It didn't feel right to him to steal it," said Bona.[41]

Also in his early teens, Wesley's work as a paperboy plus his good grades and his attendance at camp were recognized with an award presented annually to one member of the Boys' Club. He was named the Fred W. Allsopp Newsboy of the Year for his "performance as a newspaperboy, school achievement, and good citizenship."[42] This was the first of two awards he would win from the organization.

The orderly, nurturing, and innocent days that Wesley enjoyed at camp in the summer of 1959 contrasted sharply with the turmoil that embroiled Little Rock. Five years previously, the Supreme Court had ruled that racial segregation in public schools was unconstitutional in *Brown v. Board of Education*. Since then, Little Rock authorities had fought integration of its schools and, in the process, become a focal point of the civil rights struggle. At the start of the school year in 1957, nine black students were scheduled to enroll at Central High School. Governor Orval Faubus called out the Arkansas National Guard to surround the school, claiming that their presence was necessary to preserve law and order. When the black students tried to enter the school on September 4, the National Guard turned them away. Later that month, a federal judge ruled that Governor Faubus had actually used the troops to block integration, and Faubus was forced to call them off. They were replaced by the Little

Rock Police. When the nine black students finally entered the school on September 23, the mob outside grew unruly and the police escorted the students out.

The next day, President Eisenhower granted Little Rock Mayor Woodrow Mann's request for army troops to support the integration process. Within 24 hours, 1,000 members of the 101st Airborne Division and 10,000 federalized National Guard troops descended upon Central High. The black students were escorted in on September 25. The crisis continued to escalate, however, and in June 1958 the Board of Education won a ruling from Federal District Court Judge Harry Lemley to delay integration in the schools. The judge ruled that integration was delayed until 1961 because even though black students had a constitutional right to attend, the "time has not come for them to enjoy that right."[43]

Two months later, Judge Lemley's ruling was reversed on appeal. But in September, Governor Faubus made another drastic move to avoid integration and closed down all three high schools—including Hall High, from which Clark would eventually graduate—for the academic year. Voters showed their overwhelming support in a vote that tallied 7,561 for integration and 129,470 against. Thousands of students were forced to find alternatives; approximately 750 white students enrolled in the city's new, private T. J. Raney High School, and others left town to find other private or public schools.

In June 1959 the federal court ruled that the closings were unconstitutional, and the schools reopened that fall. Governor Faubus staged a protest rally at the capital on the first day of school, and 250 marchers showed up at Central High carrying American flags. Unlike the first time they faced a mob, the Little Rock police arrested some of the marchers and turned fire hoses on the rest.

Although the worst was evidently over, black and white students faced a nerve-wracking term that year. Armed guards gave the halls an atmosphere more like a federal prison than a high school. Wesley's neighbor, Patty Loveless, recalled how terrifying those first weeks were. "I went to Central for the first semester, then we moved and I transferred to Hall," she said. "National Guard men were in the halls with their guns and it was frightening. We just went on about our business as best we could."[44]

After years of legal maneuvering, protests, school board scandals, and school closings, integration in Little Rock had begun. The phase-in plan drew out the process for years, however. All grades in the public schools were not integrated until 1972. The events of the late 1950s made icons of the black students who had stepped into Central High for the first time, as they were thereafter known throughout the world as the Little Rock Nine.[45]

Wesley was in ninth grade at Pulaski Heights Junior High the year that the three high schools were closed. Like many other parents, Veneta and Victor Clark feared that the high schools would still be closed the next academic year, and they worked to find an out-of-town school for Wesley's sophomore year. As Patty Loveless remarked, "Most parents had a Plan B."[46] The Clarks' plan was Castle Heights Military Academy in Lebanon, Tennessee.

"In those days there were a lot of military schools around," said Phillip McMath, who went to Castle Heights with Wesley in 1959–1960. "They were very popular, and Castle Heights had kids enrolled from all over the world. Even though it's no longer open, at that time it was a growing operation." Phillip and Wesley spent whatever free time they had with friends from the Arkansas contingent, but military drills and sports cut into study time, which didn't leave many hours for recreation. "They kept us busy," said Phillip. "There was inspection on Saturday morning, then we had Saturday afternoon off and maybe we went to see a movie. Sunday morning we had to march to church. And we usually had a parade. And on Monday classes started again, and in the afternoon we had drills and swimming practice. We had very little down time."[47] Neither Wesley nor Phillip took to the spit-and-polish aspect of Castle Heights. "I have never enjoyed standing inspections, polishing shoes, marching in parades," said Wesley. "It just seemed like three or four hours wasted."[48]

But among the saving graces of Castle Heights, as far as Wesley was concerned, was the swimming team. Little Rock schools did not offer swimming, so if he had been attending one of the newly opened high schools back home he wouldn't swim other than at the Boys' Club. Castle Heights' sports program, however, was extensive. "Football is almost like a religion in Arkansas," said Phillip. "In Arkansas it was *the* sport. In Little Rock there was also a basketball program and a track team, but nothing else. Castle Heights, on the other hand, had wrestling and soccer and swimming and all sorts of things. Swimming was a big element of the school; we had our own pool and coach and we went all over the mid-South to swim meets. It was a first-class operation."[49]

At the end of the year, Clark was the top student in his class academically.[50] Wesley and Phillip then returned to Little Rock to enroll at Hall High School for the 1960–1961 school year. While they were in Tennessee, integration had occurred quietly at Hall. Three black girls had joined the student body of 700 white students, and although their entrance did not ignite the protests that occurred at Central, life was miserable for them at the school. Estella Johnson, for example, endured cruelties such as tacks on her chair and obscenities scrawled on her papers. In an interview with the *Boston Globe* she remarked that it was "just as life-altering and traumatic" for the three girls to integrate Hall as it had been for the nine blacks to enter Central High. She also recalled where Wesley fit into the newly integrated system. "There were three kinds of people there," she said. "Those who overtly bothered us, those who were friendly, and those who left us alone—and he left us alone."

Elsie Dodson was the only black student in Wesley's grade, and she had no white friends in the school. She went on to get a degree in nursing and worked for twenty-six years in the Veterans Administration. Her experiences as a nurse gave her apt analogies to her years at Hall High. "It is like being in a war zone, where you are around mostly enemy," she said.[51] In the same article, Wesley remarked that the integration upheavals in Little Rock were events that shaped his entire life. Decades later, during his Democratic campaign for the nomination, he elaborated on what he learned from those days and how it affected his stand on affirmative action. "Growing up in Little Rock, I saw firsthand the ugly legacy of racial discrimination," he wrote in a *Detroit Free Press* commentary. "For all of us in Little Rock, Central High School is a shrine to that struggle to end racial segregation. But the end of segregation did not mean the end of discrimination. Racial hatred has deep and pernicious roots in our nation's history. It is a cancer that needs to be cured, and affirmative action has been one of the most effective treatments."[52]

When Wesley began his junior year at Hall High, he talked to Phillip about starting a school swim team. There was no coach, no sponsorship, and no pool, but Wesley was undaunted. He volunteered to be coach and captain and suggested they could practice at the Boys' Club. Phillip agreed, and they formed the first swim team in Hall history and in the public school history of Little Rock. Wesley's skillful performance reached a high point at a state meet, when the team was scheduled for a four-man relay. One member of the relay was sick and didn't show up, so Wesley said he'd swim two legs of the relay. "When he swam the anchor leg of that relay, he was behind," Phillip said. "And he had already been in the water for an event. So there was no way he was supposed to catch those guys who were fresh. He caught them and passed them, we won the event. I was surprised by that, I was flabbergasted."[53] As a result, Wesley's desire to form a team not only provided a new sport for his classmates that year, it provided Hall High with a Big Nine championship.

Wesley and Phillip continued to swim on the Boys' Club team after they formed the high school team. Over the years, Phillip saw enough of the competition to know that Wes stood out from the pack. "We had the best swimmer in the state in Wesley Clark," he said. "He could have been an Olympic swimmer. He was top flight. He's extremely self-motivated and to this day he keeps himself in tip-top condition." But Wesley's involvement in extracurricular activities as well as his plans to go to college didn't allow for a professional pursuit of the sport. "To be an Olympic swimmer you can't do anything else," Phillip added. "When you compete at that level you've got to dedicate your life to swimming. But I think he had that potential."[54]

In addition to serving as captain of the swimming team, Wesley was president of the National Honor Society and a National Merit Semifinalist, and took honors classes in English, math, and science. He was an editor of the *Inkwell*, a literary journal run by members of the honors

English class, and selected as a member of the Key Club, Math Club, and Beta Club, a national leadership-service organization. When Hall High offered the first calculus course in the state of Arkansas during his junior year, he was among the brainy minority who signed up. It was common knowledge at Hall that Wesley was one of the smartest guys in the school. He was also good-looking— newspaper clippings and yearbook photos from those years show a handsome face with thick, dark eyebrows that set off his violet eyes, jet-black hair, and a perfect smile. (The Clarks had paid for braces when he was younger, and a junior high newsletter listed Wesley as the boy with the "best teeth" in a list of traits of the "Ideal Pulaski Heights Boy.")[55] Even though Wesley was respected and admired, the most popular boys in the school were the football and basketball stars. Although none of his friends would describe him as a "geek," Wesley hung out with more of the nonjock crowd. His thick-framed black eyeglasses contributed to his bookish look.

In his junior year, Wesley was chosen to attend the American Legion's Boys' State, a weeklong workshop in government held every year for high school juniors. Offered to only the brightest students, it was considered an honor to be selected and the program sought to instill a weighty, if not sacred sense of civic duty. Upon arrival, Wesley was assigned to a mock political party and city and participated in elections to set up a state government. Judges, political office holders, attorneys, professors, and others gave practical sessions about the jobs of public officials and the obligations of the citizens at every level of government. Like the other participants, Wesley was selected for his leadership potential (Bill Clinton would attend a couple of years later and was elected governor of the mock state). The program's creed reflects the program's goal in statements such as "American citizenship is my most priceless possession. .... It is my obligation to participate in and contribute my effort to the civic and political welfare of my community, state, and nation.... May the experience of Boys' State be ever with me as a reminder of my obligation to God and Country."[56]

The weeklong infusion of politicking and legislating at Boys' State in the summer of 1961 set Wesley up for an outstanding senior year at Hall. He continued to excel on the debate team, in which he and his partner were finalists at a major southern meet, the Waco Invitational Debate Tournament in Texas.[57] In spite of the enormous amount of preparation and travel time involved in debate, Wesley never had a problem keeping up with the rest of his work and was always in the top 10 percent of his class. Debating was in his blood by the time he graduated from Hall, and he would go on to compete on teams at West Point and Oxford University.

Another indication that Wesley's gifts were admired by his classmates came with his second-place rank in the school's Who's Who listing of Most Intellectual Boy in Our Class. And in February of that year, he received city-wide recognition with his second honor from the Boys' Club. Chosen out of 5,400 members of the club, he was named Boy of the Year for 1962. The award noted that he was selected for "the amount and quality of his service to home, school, church, community, and the Boys' Club."[58] The club's board president, James Coates Jr. presented Wesley with a plaque at the ceremony. The honor was mutual, as Wesley remarked years later, because the club not only gave him another father figure but also the opportunity to learn about himself and discover his strengths. "That's where I really learned leadership and life—from the Boys' Club," he said in 1997.[59]

In high school, Wesley also continued to attend Pulaski Heights Baptist Church, showing up twice on Sundays for the morning and evening services. His interest in religion, which had begun with weekly Bible readings at church in the first grade, had intensified through the years. "During several periods in my life I went to Baptist training union," he said. "I was a member of Royal Ambassadors for a year or so, which is the Baptists' youth group."[60] Even though his parents were not churchgoers, Wesley found a spiritual home at Pulaski Heights Baptist Church.

One of his training union teachers, Margaret Kolb, recalled that Wesley "really had a genuine spiritual depth about him. He was serious when you needed to be serious, but he wasn't pious and didn't stand out like a sore thumb or an egghead. It seemed to come natural or easy for him to be doing the right thing at the right time. He was affable, genuinely comfortable to be with, and friendly." There were about twenty boys in Wesley's training union group, which was designed to teach about how the church is run as well as about discipleship and the Christian life. They did study units on morals and ethics, and on mission fieldwork. For a lesson on missions in Kenya, for example, they would study the geography and culture of that country. Every Sunday night someone from the group would stand up and give a presentation on the part that he had been assigned the week before. "Wesley always did an excellent job; you could tell he was as smart as can be," said Kolb. "He was a delight to work with. If you wanted to be sure something got done in the right way at the right time, you asked Wes to do it."[61]

The second education arm of the church in which Wesley was involved, the Royal Ambassadors, was a boys' study group. The girls had their own named the Girls' Auxiliary. In this program the boys memorized and studied scripture, and their work was recognized by a reward system similar to the merit badges given out in Boy Scouts. They also had a recreation program and played softball in the church league at Allsop Park.

"The youth programs at our church gave Wes a very nurturing, stable, spiritual background," said Kolb. "The pastor was Dr. Harrel Hicks, a stately, dignified man and an excellent Bible scholar. His sermons were long-winded, but if Wesley was listening he learned a lot about theology. Everyone adored him because he was a wonderful family man who was very active in the community." Hicks was also a big supporter of high school football and had sons on the teams. Sometimes, when there was an away game on a Saturday night, he would get a substitute preacher for Sunday. Wesley grew up singing traditional hymns out of the Southern Baptist Hymnal as well as a scattering of old-fashioned tent revival music included in the book. "They did love to sing those old hymns that had a lot of rhythm to it," said Kolb, "but we never clapped hands in our church."[62]

The congregation at Pulaski Heights Baptist Church was all white, but there were a few black staff members who worked as janitors and cleaning ladies. During the struggles to desegregate the public schools, Margaret Kolb worked to enforce integration as did many other members of the church. She and other training mission instructors supported integration and taught their boys' classes about the moral and Christian foundations for it. "Our church was one of the ones that had people really involved in the integration crisis," she said. "I was a member of the Women's Emergency Committee for the Schools, which worked to promote integration, and Pastor Hicks supported our committee. We discussed integration with the boys in training mission." The church congregation, like the city of Little Rock, was divided on the issue. "You had to do everything you could to come up on people's blind side," Kolb said, "and let them see why integration was important. Ours was one of the churches that struggled with it, even though there were those in the church who didn't believe in it. It was very difficult because we had two or three deacons who said 'If any of those black people come and try to visit our church we'll be nice to them, but we'll tell them that we'll be glad to take them over to Mt. Zion Baptist.'"[63]

Kolb recalled a luncheon that was arranged to honor all the church staff, including the black employees and their families. "We had some who didn't stay for lunch that Sunday," she said. "It had never occurred to them to eat in the same room as blacks." She also recalled an evening when Pastor Hicks brought some black students to the Wednesday night church meal, and two white men got up and left. But those who stood for integration and placed editorials and ads in the paper to help promote it did not waver. "All of us were working in that direction because it had been part of our Christian training," she said, "but some of us had to take the lead."[64]

Wesley witnessed the slow process of integration in Little Rock in his church, school system, and the Boys' Club. Black boys finally had the opportunity to go to camp in 1958, but these encampments were held at separate times and run by their own staff, completely segregated from the white camp. And the Kiwanis Club collected most of its operating budget for the Boys' Club camp through a fundraiser that propagated one of the worst stereotypes of a bygone era. At each Annual Kiwanis Minstrel Show, Kiwanis members wore blackface makeup as they sang and danced in two-night musical revues patterned after the nineteenth-century minstrel shows. The Kiwanis shows were very popular and ran from the mid-1930s through 1974.[65]

The Boys' Club camp, which was such an important part of Wesley's childhood, is a microcosm of the social change that has occurred in Little Rock and the country. Today, the Joseph Pfeifer Kiwanis Camp is an extraordinarily successful school program directed by black educator Sanford Tollette. The camp provides a year-round education for children at risk, both black and white, combining traditional academics with nature study and outdoor activities. In 1998, the camp received the Organization of the Year Award from the Association for Experiential Education.

During his campaign in 2003–2004, Wesley talked about his southern roots and his love for the land that he developed on vacations at his Aunt Jewel's cabin, hunting with his stepfather, and camping at the Boys' Club camp. He talked about his values and how they were formed by his teachers and mentors in Little Rock. "What it all comes down to is that I am who I am because of what I learned right here in the South," he said in his "True Grits Tour" kickoff speech. He holds fond memories of the camp that lured him back as a counselor in the summers when he was a cadet at West Point.

When Wesley Clark retired from the army in 2000, he moved back to Little Rock, and if he were to drive out to the old camp he would find that some physical elements have deteriorated, while others have survived. Little Maumelle Creek still runs through the acreage, but the water is too polluted for swimming and campers now take lessons in an in-ground pool. Children still bed down in the old stone-and-wood cabins beneath the towering pines. And although the Red Bridge is gone, there's still a deep spot in the creek near the road.

THREE

✯ ✯ ✯ ✯

"The Corps, the Corps, and the Corps"

> "You are the leaven which binds together the entire fabric of our national system of defense.... The Long Gray Line has never failed us. Were you to do so, a million ghosts in olive drab, in brown khaki, in blue and gray, would rise from their white crosses thundering those magic words: duty, honor, country."
> —Gen. Douglas MacArthur to
> West Point cadets, 1962[1]

Clark's attendance at Boys' State in the summer of 1961 turned out to be much more than an academic honor and introduction to government. By the end of that week, he knew where he wanted to go to college, what career he wanted to follow, and why. There were several uniformed West Point cadets at the event, invited by the American Legion to act as counselors. Most of them were from Arkansas, and they wore an air of confidence and prestige that impressed even that crop of high-achieving teenagers. One of the cadets captured Clark's attention, and they discussed the opportunities presented by the academy. That conversation answered a lot of questions that Clark had been asking himself for years, about how to best be of service to his country and which of many interests to follow professionally. "I remember walking out of there and telling [classmate] Jerry Bona, 'OK, that's where I'm going. I'm going to West Point,'" he said.[2]

Clark had developed his desire to serve his country throughout his childhood in the Cold War years, listening to MacArthur's speech about communism, watching the news about *Sputnik*, and being moved by Kennedy's call to win the space race and put a man on the moon. He dreamed of joining the navy or another branch of the military that could teach him to fly and set him on the path of becoming an astronaut. But these hopes vanished when he discovered that he didn't have perfect eyesight, which was a requirement for flyers. He learned about his nearsightedness one day in his junior year while driving some of the Boys' Club swim team to a meet in Bartlesville, Oklahoma. "I had just turned sixteen and I was really happy to drive," he said. A sign came up that looked fuzzy, but he assumed it looked that way to everyone until someone read it. "I thought everybody couldn't see that sign. I guess that's when my eyes went bad."[3]

He resigned himself to the fact that the military was no longer an option—until he met the cadet at Boys' State. It was not so much what the cadet had to say that convinced him—everyone knew that West Point was one of the top schools in the country and a prestigious starting point for a military career—but the fact that the cadet was wearing glasses. In that conversation, Clark learned that he didn't need 20/20 vision to attend the United States Military Academy at West Point or to serve in the army, and he made up his mind in a heartbeat. "It was my belief in service that led me to West Point," he said. "It was the year after John F. Kennedy admonished us to ask not what our country could do for us, but what we could do for our country."[4]

Clark's first step in getting to the academy was obtaining a nomination from a member of Congress or the Department of the Army, which every cadet must receive. His family didn't have any political connections, so he had no choice but to try getting the congressional appointment on his own. First, he wrote a letter to Arkansas Senator J. William Fulbright. When he didn't receive a response, he traveled to Washington, DC, to make his case in person to other congressmen. Clark, now a sixteen-year-old senior, did not expect the gruff reception he received from Arkansas Senator John L. McClellan. When he stepped into McClellan's imposing office in the Donaghey Building, the senator stayed in his chair and began shooting questions. "He was an older man behind a huge desk," Clark said. "He didn't stand up, and he said, 'I understand you want to go to West Point.' I said, 'Yessir, yessir I do.'

"He said, 'Boy, how old are you?' I said, 'Well, I'm sixteen years old.'

"He said, 'How much do you weigh?' I said, 'I weigh 138 pounds.'

"He said, 'Do you make good grades?' I said, 'Yes, senator, I do.'

"He said, 'How good?' I said, 'Well, I make straight A's at Hall High School.'

"He said, 'You're not old enough, you're not big enough and you're not smart enough to go to West Point. Come back and maybe talk to me next year.'"[5]

After failing to get a senatorial nomination, Clark turned to a House member. One of his stepfather's friends back in Little Rock knew Representative Dale Alford, and he was able to set up an appointment with him. Alford had received other requests from Arkansas seniors who wanted to apply to West Point, and was at a loss as to how to choose among them. He decided to make each of them take the civil service test and said that he would grant his nomination to whomever got the highest score. Clark took the test in December and learned one month later that he earned the top score. In January, Alford signed the nomination, and on February 28, Clark traveled to Fort Leonard Wood, Missouri, where the academic and physical entrance exams to West Point were administered. His academic qualifications would be measured by the college board examinations as well as by his past academic record. His physical aptitude, according to the letter from army headquarters, would be tested "to measure coordination, strength, agility, and other physical attributes." The notice added that "advance preparation is recommended for all candidates." The testing was over on March 3, and he returned home. Seven weeks later, he received the letter. *Dear Mr. Clark: You have been selected for admission and are authorized to report to the United States Military Academy, West Point. . . .* The letter added that his entrance to the academy was a life-changing commitment that demanded his "serious thought":

> You are to be congratulated on this opportunity for admission to the Military Academy, for it comes only to a select few of America's youth. It presents a challenge that will demand your best effort. Therefore, it is suggested that you give serious thought to your desire for a military career as, without proper motivation, you may find it difficult to conform to what may be a new way of life.[6]

The sense of gravity surrounding this life choice was made greater by a tragedy concerning another West Point hopeful from Little Rock that year. David Murphree, a barber's son who attended the boys' study groups at

Pulaski Heights Baptist Church, also waited anxiously for his letter in the spring of 1962. In April he received notice that his application to the academy was denied. The news devastated him, and he took his own life using a rifle in his home. Margaret Kolb, who taught Murphree and Clark at the church, recalled the conversations she had with her husband, a psychiatrist, about the suicide. "Teenagers are so emotional, when they are heartbroken they will do something on the spur on the moment," she said. She and her husband mourned the fact that there was a gun in the boy's house, and continue to wonder if he would have overcome his suicidal thoughts with time.[7]

Clark was drawn to West Point as a place that would start him on the road to serving his country, a path he had considered from the time he realized *Sputnik* beeped overhead. It was also a deeply imbedded issue about where he was from. He called it "a southern thing, to be drawn to the concept of service to country. . . . It was just a belief that this was the right thing to do, to be an army officer. It was not romantic. . . . West Point was simply a means to an end."[8] He won a National Merit Scholarship in high school and was offered full scholarships at Ivy League schools including Harvard and Yale, but he wasn't interested. A Harvard recruiter tried to talk to him about the university, but Clark wouldn't see him. "I said, 'No, I want to go to West Point,'" Clark recalled. Tuition was free for every cadet at West Point, and Clark would also receive $111.15 per month to cover the cost of his uniforms, textbooks, and incidentals. It would have been difficult for the Clarks to fund their son's education otherwise; they were not well off enough to pay for an Ivy League education. "Both my parents were a little embarrassed the way things turned out," Clark said. "They didn't socialize, they worked. . . . Neither one of them felt like they'd lived up to their financial potential, and it was a struggle for them."[9]

In July 1962, two months before the start of the academic year, Clark arrived at West Point, which at that time did not admit women, with other new cadets to go through the academy's grueling rite-of-passage known as Beast Barracks. Officially named New Cadet Barracks, this training camp earned its popular name in the decades after the Civil War, when a separate hazing period for new cadets was formed. Beast Barracks is the academy's crash course for turning civilians into cadets and ultimately army officers, and those who don't make the cut are weeded out before the fall term begins. The new students are indoctrinated into the Fourth Class System, where upperclassmen have the right to discipline lower classmen. Most of the disciplining is done to the plebes/freshmen, also known as fourth classmen. Sophomores are known as yearlings, juniors as cows, and seniors as firsties. The class system—including the harsh treatment of new cadets—is central to the academy's organizational philosophy. Its three functions were "the conversion of a young man into a professional soldier, the identification of those cadets who cannot function under stress, and the provision of a vehicle by which upperclasses can improve their leadership techniques."[10] Freshmen entering West Point were the smartest boys in their high schools and accustomed to being respected, admired, and standing out both intellectually and athletically. Beast Barracks was designed to wipe that slate clean and instill instant obedience. New cadets were put under mental and physical stress around the clock and would not become part of the corps of cadets until they passed this two-month initiation.

The moment Clark entered the academy as a new

cadet on July 2, 1962, his life was under the absolute control of upperclassmen who barked orders and demanded that he brace—pull his head down into his shoulders. From Beast Barracks through their first year, plebes had to assume the brace posture everywhere except in their rooms. Plebes were forced to memorize hundreds of lines of trivia, which upperclassmen would test them on at mealtime in Washington Hall. If a new cadet did not know "plebe knowledge," such as how many gallons of water were held in Lusk Reservoir, his plate would be taken away. In clothing formations, they were ordered to change into specific uniforms on a moment's notice, which sent them rushing through their manuals trying to figure out the codes for different sets of clothing. Shower hazing included being forced to do push-ups while holding a bar of soap in one hand, and at any time a new cadet could be ordered to do deep knee bends while flailing his arms (Eagling) or drop facedown into the dirt and pump his legs and arms (Swimming to Newburgh). The hazings could occur at any time, which added to the pressure of the scheduled training in which they learned how to march, present arms, and shoot an M-14.

On his first evening of Beast Barracks, Clark and his fellow new cadets signed a paper stating that they would serve at least four years in the army after graduation. The road ahead appeared especially long for Clark, who had already decided after a year at Castle Heights that he didn't like the drills of military school.

Stress and food deprivation caused new cadets to lose weight during those first two months and throughout their plebe year. Clark was already small at 144 pounds (and nearing his present height of 5'10") when he showed up for Beast Barracks, and in the first week he lost 15 pounds. His hazing experiences included an incident down in the basement shower area known as the "sinks," when a group of upperclassmen gathered around him. One of them yelled into his face, "You better throw your head back, you better suck in that chin, you hear me?" With the cadet's face only an inch from his own, and embarrassed to be wearing only a thin cotton robe, Clark could not suppress a smirk. At that offense, his tormenters pushed him into a foot-wide locker, locked him in and knocked it from side to side, forcing his head to slam against the clothing hooks inside. They refused to let him out until a sympathetic firstie came along and ordered them to let him go.[11]

Clark survived the academy's first rite of passage and became a member of the class of 1966. He was assigned to company B-4, where he roomed with Theodore Hill, a native New Yorker and fellow math wizard. Beast Barracks had not dampened Clark's self-confidence; when he met Hill he announced, "I'm going to be number one in the class." He meant it, and Hill admired his confidence. Soon, everyone would see Clark's goal become a reality. At West Point, class seating was arranged according to academic rank. The cadet with the highest grade—first in class—sat in the first chair in the front row, the second next to him, and so on. From physics to English, Clark was almost always in that first corner seat, and Hill was close by. This system made it easy to detect the highest academic achievers, and they were targeted for it. "I remember he would be angry at some of the people who went out of their way to harass him because he was doing well academically, or didn't think he was macho enough," Hill said. "Wes is not one of these back-slapping, everybody-is-my-buddy types.

He is a private person. I think some people were just intimidated by his intellectual power. But I loved it. We talked for hours."[12]

The program at West Point led to a bachelor of science degree, and Clark's course schedule each semester included academic classes, physical education, and military science courses (tactics). All but six elective courses were part of a standard academic program, and cadets spent approximately 59 percent of their time on academic subjects and 41 percent on military coursework.[13] The 1962–1963 West Point catalogue stated that the cadet's education must be broad and encompass both the sciences and the humanities. "An officer in the United States Army must be a man of high character, a trained leader, a clear thinker, and a versatile scholar.... He must possess a depth of knowledge that will qualify him to pursue graduate studies in any area which the needs of the military service may dictate. The curriculum of the Military Academy is designed to produce such an officer."[14] Heavy with science courses, the curriculum at West Point was similar to an engineering program at other schools, with additional training in military science and tactics.

As a freshman, Clark had mathematics class every day, Monday through Saturday; engineering fundamentals, environment, English, and foreign languages (he took Russian) three days per week; tactics twice a week; and physical education on a varied schedule.

As a sophomore, he added physics, chemistry, history, and a course called psychology and methods of instruction. For at least one course, chemistry, Clark was able to enroll in the advanced section because he had already mastered most of the material covered in the standard class. Because there were so many courses, half of the classes met on Saturdays as well as during the week.

In his junior year, Clark studied mechanics of fluids, mechanics of solids, electrical science, economics, and law, as well as the standard tactics and physical education. Tactics courses over the four-year program included training in the weapons and organization of the infantry and other companies, map reading, night-and-day patrolling exercises, large-scale military problems, and orientation trips to the U.S. Army Armor Center at Fort Knox, Kentucky, and other bases.

Senior year included civil engineering, history of military art, ordnance engineering, leadership, and a course on international relations.

A typical day started with reveille at 6:05 a.m., breakfast from 6:45 to 7:15, scheduled study from 7:15 to 7:55, and more classes and study hours until lunch at 12:10. In the afternoon, classes, parades, extracurriculars, and athletics were punctuated by two breaks called "unscheduled times": one lasting ten minutes and another twenty. Cadets poured into Washington Hall for supper hour at 6:20, and study time was scheduled from 7:15 to 9:30. At 10:00, the bugle rang out "Taps," and lights out was called at 11:00.

Clark's grades were excellent, putting him in the top 5 percent of his class every year. This classified him as a Distinguished Cadet, signified by a five-pointed star on both sides of his uniform collar. John Wheeler, a fellow member of the class of 1966, recalled that it was because of him that Clark didn't take the top spot in Russian class his freshman year. "I walked away with the prize in Russian," Wheeler said, explaining that he had an advantage because of the book they were assigned to use. "The textbook we were using as plebes was the one I had used for Russian in high school the previous year," he said. "We marched through that book the same way; we did the drill. We memorized every little conversation, 'We eat black bread and cheese.' Wes was used to being number one in everything; he worked and achieved it. But he finished second in Russian. It wasn't disabling or irritating, it just bothered him."[15]

Wheeler also recalled a conversation he had one day with Clark about reading and studying. "He would read some books in a matter of minutes, in less than an hour," Wheeler said. "I remember that conversation distinctly. I asked him, in particular, how long it took him to read *Darkness at Noon*. He told me, 'Not that long, about forty-five minutes.' I also learned that his study time was about thirty minutes, some time late in the evening, as opposed to about three-and-a-half hours spent by every other cadet."[16]

By the time Clark had taken several math and science courses, he was uncertain how he would apply pure science to his military career. An elective course during his sophomore year helped him find a more satisfying direction. "I had no experience in international affairs before, but I took a social science course . . . which absolutely grabbed me. So that all fit," he said.[17]

Although the academy's academic program was very rigorous, Clark spent many hours per week in extracurricular activities. He was on the swimming team the first two years, in the scuba club as a junior and senior, and on the pistol, cross-country, and squash teams at various times. He served on public information detail for two years and Russian club for one year, and also continued his religious studies as a member of the academy's Baptist Student Union for three years. But far more time-consuming was his work on the Debate Council, which he joined in his sophomore, junior, and senior years. According to the academy catalogue, debate gave cadets "the opportunity of acquiring skills in public speaking and in the use of logic, and of using and perfecting these skills in tournament debating in competition with colleges and universities throughout the country." Clark set an academy record for trips away from the school as a member of the Debate Council. His yearbook states, "As a cadet, Wes has probably taken more trips than the Glee Club." He considered it an opportunity to get away from the regimented grind of the academy. "That was a great way to get out of West Point on weekends," he said. "I set the record for number of days away from West Point. You have to live a balanced life."[18]

Jack LeCuyer, Clark's debate partner, recalled one very long stretch away from school. "When we were first classmen we left in the last weekend in October to debate in Chicago, and between then and the first of the year we were at West Point a total of eight days, four of which were Thanksgiving vacation," he said. "I think people envied us because we weren't there a lot. They didn't realize it was hard work. We were always high finishers and we won many best speaker awards. We debated in the national debate tournament two years running."[19]

LeCuyer credits forensics with a lot of the skills that both he and Clark found helpful throughout their careers. "When Wes and I debated, all the topics were domestic issues, such as 'Should Seat Belts Be Mandatory?' and other interesting social problems. Debate teaches you to think, to marshal your evidence to make your point or refute a point. It teaches you very clearly the art of listening, because if you don't listen to what the other side is saying, you're not going to do well as far as refutation or making your case. The art of listening, of assembling a lot of information, and thinning it down to the relevant points, teaches you how to be persuasive without being argumentative."[20]

Clark's debating schedule came to the attention of one army officer who didn't think the cadet was striking the right balance in his academic career. One of the debate coaches, William Taylor, got a phone call one day from another West Point instructor, Capt. Norman Schwarzkopf. "I don't like what you are doing with cadet Wes Clark," he told Taylor. "He is not competing with varsity athletics. He is not socializing with the rest of his classmates. He is off doing debate tournaments. You are undermining the professionalism of this young man."

"I don't know who you are," Taylor responded, and proceeded to give Schwarzkopf a quick rundown of the virtues of debate and hung up the phone.[21] The coach had a great team—West Point was well-known as a top college debating school—and Clark, one of the best, was Chairman of the Debate Council. His sophomore year, for example, Clark and his debate partner won all five debates in the National Novice Debate Tournament at Dartmouth College, and Clark also nabbed another trophy as Best Public Speaker.[22] Taylor had no doubts about Clark's professionalism. As far as athletics were concerned, he knew that Clark was more than holding his own, too. He was coach of his regimental triathlon team and high point scorer in the regimental 1965–1966 intramurals.[23]

Taking advanced classes and competing on the national level in debate were two challenging aspects of the academy for Clark, and some of the coursework also deepened his concept of public service and gave him an idea of how soldiers have been perceived throughout history. In philosophy class, Clark discovered Plato's concept of the soldier as a spirited protector of society who cared more about the nation than about himself. It is the responsibility of these men of spirit, or silver, as Plato called them in the *Republic*, to dedicate their passion for their country into defending it. Their philosophy teacher, Lt. Gen. Dale Vesser, recalled that Clark took Plato's ideas to heart rather than simply going through the motions to get a good grade. Clark genuinely wanted to see soldiering in the context of a noble civic duty, based on the idea, as Vesser described it, that "one acquires obligations because one has talents that need to be employed for society." [24]

John Wheeler was in this class with Clark, and recalled that it was a close-knit, "high octane" class. "When we got to this Platonic idea of the men of brass, silver, or gold, I, like most others in the class, thought we were supposed to be philosopher-kings, men of gold. Wes saw that it wasn't about gold, but about silver—the men of silver protect the state. He understood the responsibility of being a dedicated soldier and a guardian of the state. It took some insight, and Wes had not only brilliance, but maturity." Wheeler also observed that their teacher, Vesser, had an enormous impact on Clark. "He was Clark's mentor," he said. "He was the coolest guy." Wheeler remembered the spring day that Vesser took the class outside to discuss philosophy while sitting on the grass. "We all trooped outside and sat around a chestnut tree in Kosciusko's Garden," he said. "It was just memorable. We had never seen such a thing at West Point, and Vesser later got his knuckles rapped for it. Wes was laughing and enjoying it; we were all busy chewing the fat and looking like we were talking about philosophy. Vesser was a Rhodes scholar out of the class of 1954. When it came time to choose which branch of the army we wanted to serve in, Clark went armor because guess who had been armor? Vesser."[25]

Vesser had been a Rhodes scholar, the army fellow at Harvard, and would go on to serve a total of thirty-three years of active service in the army, including two tours in Vietnam, where combat duty earned him the Silver Star, Distinguished Flying Cross, Purple Heart, and Air Medal. "Clark was one of the best students it was my good fortune to teach in my years at the academy," Vesser said. "He always was highly motivated and competitive, both as a cadet and as an officer. The West Point education is a socialization process in which people become more responsible as they grow, and he certainly took to heart the ideals not only of West Point but of those aspects of his education that he chose to value." Vesser recalled that Clark integrated what he learned to help him find his place in the world and make decisions about how he would live his life. "I think he'd always been interested in learning what you can know and what you have to believe. As one looks for signposts in what is a puzzling world, young people look to different things, and several of us think that the great philosophers like Plato have had much to say about what's of value and how one can live his or her life."[26]

Clark was one of perhaps two or three cadets whom Vesser considered his intellectual superiors among the several hundred cadets he taught at West Point. "It's humbling to acknowledge that somebody you're teaching is brighter than you are or that he's a better writer," he said.[27] In the future, Clark's career would in some ways echo Vesser's; he would also win the Silver Star for combat in Vietnam, teach economics and coach debate at

West Point, and serve as J5 in the Joint Chiefs of Staff office in Washington.

Another important influence on Clark's idea of a military calling was Gen. Douglas MacArthur's famous West Point speech, given on May 12, 1962, in acceptance of the Sylvanus Thayer Award. This would be the general's last public speech, as he died less than two years later, and it contained rousing sentiments about army life that have been memorized by cadets ever since. The speech, given just weeks before Clark's class arrived, had been recorded, and Clark's incoming group of new cadets were assembled in an auditorium during Beast Barracks to listen to it.[28] MacArthur's impassioned, uplifting message gave the class a new perspective on their roles as future officers, and boosted their morale during those hellish first weeks:

> Duty, honor, country. Those three hallowed words reverently dictate what you ought to be, what you can be, what you will be. They are your rallying points: to build courage when courage seems to fail; to regain faith when there seems to be little cause for faith; to create hope when hope becomes forlorn. . . . They build your basic character, they mold you for your future roles as the custodians of the nation's defense. . . . They create in your heart the sense of wonder, the unfailing hope of "what next," and the joy and inspiration of life. They teach you in this way to be an officer and a gentleman. . . .
>
> The code which those words perpetuate embraces the highest moral laws and will stand the test of any ethics or philosophies ever promulgated for the uplift of mankind. . . . The soldier, above all other men, is required to practice the greatest act of religious training—sacrifice. . . .
>
> Yours is the profession of arms—the will to win,

the sure knowledge that in war there is no substitute for victory; that if you lose, the nation will be
destroyed; that the very obsession of your public
service must be duty, honor, country.

The general concluded with a moving farewell, stating that his last thoughts before death would be of "the
corps, and the corps, and the corps."[29] Clark would hear
this speech many times over the next four years. Joining
the army began to feel like a higher calling to the cadets,
while outside the stone walls of West Point the country
reeled from one crisis to another. In the first weeks of
Clark's plebe year, President Kennedy stood his ground
against Khrushchev in the Cuban missile crisis. Thirteen
months later, Kennedy was assassinated. In 1965,
President Johnson ordered a buildup of American troops
and a massive bombing campaign in Vietnam, and the
anti-war movement raged to a new level on college campuses.

In the summer, cadets continued their military tactics
training but were given leave for a month in June. When
Clark went home to Little Rock for those long breaks, he
usually spent a week or two as a counselor at the Boys'
Club camp. He also returned during holiday breaks, and
on those visits Little Rock organizations invited him to
speak about his experiences at the academy. He had
become a local hero with his West Point appointment,
and these homecomings were sometimes full of decorum.
During his sophomore year, for example, he spent spring
break in Little Rock delivering a speech, "What West
Point Means to Me," at high schools, the Kiwanis Club,
the Arkansas State Teachers College, and other civic
clubs. He was greeted at the airport by a band of army
personnel and "Miss City Beautiful," paid a visit to
Governor Faubus at the state capitol, and did interviews

on local radio and TV stations.[30] Home for Christmas in 1965, he spoke to the Little Rock Optimist Club, which had invited local students to attend and meet the cadet. When asked what he thought about the anti-war demonstrations around the country, Clark did not give the conservative reply they may have expected from someone who had signed on to serve in the army. "People in the United States have always had the right to demonstrate," he told them, and added that demonstrations are part of American democracy. He also told the group that he was ambitious and hoped, like every cadet, to be a general one day. He clarified that his colleagues did not make an issue of those ambitions, however, explaining that "One does not talk about his military plans since we are in competition (for rank) with each other."[31]

The summer after his sophomore year, Clark got permission to spend more than two months on a trip to Europe with a classmate. They left in late June for a four-week stay in Germany, followed by a trip to Russia where Clark practiced the language in Moscow, Leningrad, and Kiev. They then traveled to Copenhagen, Amsterdam, Paris, and the French Riviera.[32]

Among his frequent travels back home for the debate team during the academic year, Clark was especially grateful when a debate trip took him to New York City. In 1964 he met his future wife, Gertrude "Gert" Kingston, at a dance in the city. She had been cajoled by her father into going to a USO dance set up for navy personnel. Mr. Kingston asked her to go as a favor to his secretary, a USO volunteer who was responsible for finding dance partners for the servicemen that evening. "I told my father I probably wouldn't want to meet anyone from the military," Gert told a reporter in 1997. Her father asked her if she would consider going for just an hour, just to make his secretary happy. "I said, 'Yessir, I'll go for an hour.' And here we are thirty-three years later."[33] Clark and some other cadets crashed the navy dance that night, and he broke the ice with Gert by complaining about his drink. "I asked for a Manhattan, and this is what they gave me," he told the attractive blonde standing nearby. "That *is* a Manhattan," she replied. Clark silently berated himself: "She was probably thinking, 'Who is this guy? He doesn't even know what's in a drink!'"[34]

Gert Kingston was working as a staff assistant for the Rothschild Brokerage House on Wall Street and going to college part-time. A native of Brooklyn, she grew up in Park Slope as the second of six children—five girls and one boy—in what she described as "a typical Irish Catholic family." Her father, Donald, worked for Catholic Charities, the social services organization, and her mother, Margaret, stayed home to raise the children and did volunteer work. "She was the great role model of my life," said Gert. "She might not have had a lot of degrees, but she had a lot of wisdom." Gert had graduated from St. Michael's Academy, an all-girls' high school on Manhattan's West Side. She had also taken courses at the Drake Secretarial and Business School, which helped her land her job at Rothschild.[35]

In his junior year at West Point, Clark's grades were still outstanding, but he broke his first-in-class ranking by coming as the number-three man (out of 589) in the General Order of Merit released in June 1965. He had been first in the order in both his freshman and sophomore years, and his combined grade average for all three years still put him in the number-one spot for the Three-Year Cumulative Order of Merit. At graduation in 1966, Clark—now captain of Company B-4—was back on top as the number-one man on the General Order of Merit.

The top academic performer in his class, Clark was slated to receive several honors during the award ceremony held on the day before graduation. But on June 7, the day of the presentation, Clark woke up with sore eyes. He went to the academy hospital and was diagnosed with "corneal abrasions of both eyes," apparently from over-wearing his contact lenses the day before. His eyes were covered in thick white bandages, and the doctor wouldn't allow him to get out of bed. Victor Clark went to the ceremony and proudly accepted his son's awards, and later Supt. Maj. Gen. Donald V. Bennett put together a personal presentation in Clark's hospital room. Victor, Veneta, and Gert stood by as Bennett congratulated the pajama-clad number-one man in the class of 1966. Clark's hospital story made the *New York Times*, complete with a photo of the heavily bandaged cadet flanked by Bennett standing by the left of his bed and his parents by the right.

Clark's six awards upon graduation were the Francis Vinton Greene Memorial Award (a set of books), Peruvian Army Award (a plaque), and U.S. Armor Association Saber Award for his number-one class standing; the General William A. Mitchell Award (another set of books) for the highest grades in military art and engineering and military history; a wristwatch, presented by the consul general of Switzerland for his excellence in debating; and a silver cigarette box, presented by the Society of the Daughters of the U.S. Army, for highest marks in advanced chemistry.

In February of Clark's senior year, his class gathered together in South Auditorium to officially select which branch of the army they would serve in—infantry, armor, artillery, signal, or engineering. Rank, as usual, determined the order of this process, and Clark was the first to stand and declare his choice: "Armor!"

In *The Long Gray Line*, Rick Atkinson's classic book about the class of 1966, the author described the auditorium's reaction after Clark made his call: "His classmates responded with a cascade of cheers and catcalls, which continued through each selection," he wrote. The class of 1966 became legendary for losing thirty cadets in Vietnam, more than any other class at West Point, and Atkinson's book is a close-up portrait of a handful of the cadets (not Clark) from their first days in Beast Barracks to their battles in Vietnam and later at home.[36]

Clark was not certain that he would get to command an armor division in the war; the jungle was not good turf for tanks and other heavy artillery. But he would take whatever orders the army handed out two years down the road, after he had finished his next academic milestone.

✯ ✯ ✯ ✯

FOUR

The Million-Dollar Wound

"Vietnam emphasizes that the Communist bloc persists in its ... long-range strategic objective of dominating the world."
—U.S. Army Lt. Col. Vernon Pizer (Ret.), 1967[1]

In James Hilton's novel *Lost Horizon*, the High Lama asks the stranded visitor, Conway, if the Western world can offer anything close to the beauty and serenity of Shangri-La. The world-weary diplomat answers with a smile, "Well, yes, to be quite frank it reminds me very slightly of Oxford."

Thirty-two Americans are selected to attend Oxford each year on a scholarship established by British philanthropist Cecil Rhodes in 1903. The prestige of attending comes from the university's centuries-long history of attracting renowned scholars as well as the historical significance of being the oldest English-speaking university in the world. Oxford was already well-established when it was hailed as the preeminent institution of learning in Europe in the fourteenth century. Clark was eligible to apply from the Gulf district, which included several southern states, and he learned in December of his senior year at West Point that he was one of the four winners from that region.

When Clark graduated from the academy, he

received his commission as a second lieutenant in the U.S. Army. Before heading to Oxford in the fall, he spent part of the summer at Fort Benning, Georgia, in the Army Airborne School. Every day, for three weeks, the soldiers started the day with warm-up exercises and a 2.4- to 4-mile run in formation. For the next seven hours they went through a rigorous, repetitive physical program that built up the trainees' confidence to jump out of a plane in flight. The first week dealt with ground training, the second week practicing jumps from a tower, and the third week making actual jumps from a plane. The program also aimed at developing leadership, "self-confidence, and an aggressive spirit through mental and physical conditioning." Clark earned his Parachutist Badge after completing five successful jumps in the last week of the course.

That summer he also spent a few weeks in New York working in a "poverty program" and visiting Gert and the Kingston family. He later told a group in Little Rock that New York's community service efforts in poverty-stricken areas did not stand up to the work done in his hometown. "I spent the summer in New York working in the poverty program in an area where community leaders and adults don't get together and do things to help the children," he told the Little Rock Kiwanis Club. "The results of this were clearly evident. The neighborhoods were terrible and the children needed care. To come back to Little Rock and see everyone doing so much and hear all the good things is very touching. I commend you for your good work."[2] At that meeting he received three awards from the city in recognition of his graduation from West Point. The City Manager Board gave him a key to the city, Pulaski County Judge Arch Campbell presented him with a document that made him a "Count of

Pulaski," and the Boys' Club gave him an Arkansas Traveler Certificate, which urges the bearer to speak well of the state wherever he goes. His next trip was across the ocean aboard the *Queen Elizabeth*, on his way to Oxford with thirty-one other Rhodes scholarship winners.

Clark attended Oxford's Magdalen College from October 1966 to August 1968, where he took the Philosophy, Politics, and Economics (PPE) program. Although this is a three-year undergraduate program, it is much more specialized and in-depth than an American curriculum and more resembles an American M.A. Clark earned a B.A. at the end of two years but, as was customary for students who already had a bachelor's degree, it was changed to an M.A. Oxford's tutorial system is unique in that candidates "reading" for the degree do not attend classes but work independently, guided by a tutor. Clark was required to write eight papers for the degree and to take written essay exams at the end of each term. For their final assessment, students receive either first (top 10 percent of the class), second, or third honors. Unlike West Point, where grades were posted frequently and classes were very structured, Clark's Oxford experience demanded that he structure his own learning. "You have to motivate yourself and put the structure in place on your own, and learn how to pursue ideas," said Stewart Early, Clark's friend and fellow Rhodes scholar. "Wes is a very disciplined guy, but I'm sure he felt the difference going from West Point to Oxford."[3]

Early was a student at Brasenose College, and he swam with Clark on the Oxford Swim Team. "I think for Clark, Oxford represented an opportunity to read a lot about politics, about leadership and philosophy," he said. "We would get together often with a few other students and talk about what we were reading, about the philosophy of life, and he really enjoyed those kinds of discussions." Usually there were four: Clark, Early, and two of Early's friends, a British student named Robin Janvrin and a New Zealander, S. Murray Boldt. "The four of us talked and explored ideas, just debating and sharing perspectives and challenging each other," said Early. "Wes really enjoyed that. We all came from different perspectives. He enjoys the intellectual exploration and listening to what everyone has to say, but on the other hand he pushes himself incredibly hard."[4]

Swimming at Oxford was not a big sport, and Clark and Early were the only Americans on the team. The university didn't have a pool, so they practiced at the Cowley City Baths, where their time was restricted to forty-five minutes three times a week. Early recalled that the end of their practice time coincided with closing time at the British Leland Assembly Plant, when thousands of workers poured into the streets on their bicycles. Clark and Early rode bikes everywhere, too, and always joined the throng.

Oxford was a formal place, and even though Clark fit in most of the time, occasionally the Arkansas boy came through. Early recalled one such moment that took place at a black-tie affair for the swim team in London. "After the Oxford-Cambridge swimming meet there was a formal dinner—you had a lot of dinners like that at Oxford—but this was a dinner in London for the team. We were sitting around enjoying dinner, and at the end of the meal Wes reached into his tuxedo pocket and took out a cigar. It was odd, because he never smoked, but he was feeling good. He tried to light it up, but the cigar had been in the pocket for a long time—it had probably been ironed over a few times. It completely disintegrated in his hand."[5]

In June 1967, after the end of his first year at Oxford, Clark traveled to New York to marry Gert Kingston. He would have married her earlier, but Rhodes scholarship rules required him to be a bachelor during his first year in the program.[6] Gert had moved to England in the spring of that year and lived with a married couple Clark knew well, U.S. Army Capt. Alex Hottell and his wife. Hottell was a West Point graduate from the class of 1964, and was currently a Rhodes scholar. After the wedding in the States, the couple returned to Oxford and set up an apartment near the university. In the same month of their marriage, the entire West Point Class of 1966 was collectively promoted to first lieutenant. This raised Clark's army salary from $303 to $504 a month and, combined with his Rhodes stipend, gave the newlyweds a comfortable life.[7] There was even enough money for Clark to splurge on a Morgan, the quintessential British sports car, handmade in a small factory in Worcestershire. They enjoyed inviting friends to tag along when they took the white roadster out for leisurely drives to London. On one drive with Gert, however, Clark had an accident and rolled the car. They walked away with nothing more than a few scrapes, but the car was totalled and towed away.

The Clarks also loved to host small dinner parties and meet new people. From the start, they had a strong relationship, and Clark gives Gert credit for helping him get through the difficult anti-American periods without becoming cynical. "A lot of people went through a lot of tension in the sixties," he said. "A lot of guilt. A lot of bitterness. I really didn't. I have my wife to thank for that. When you're settled personally ... I think it solves a lot."[8]

In his second year, Clark participated in university-sponsored debates about American involvement in

Vietnam. Anti-American sentiment over the war ran high in Great Britain, especially on college campuses, and Clark was usually the only American who agreed to participate and defend the nation's policies. "He was like the Lone Ranger," said Phillip McMath, Clark's friend from Little Rock. "He was the only American there defending American policy in Vietnam and at least one time it got out of hand." McMath recalled a story Clark told him about one debate: "People were screaming and shouting, but they managed to calm it down and turn it into a civilized, robust debate."[9]

As the only defender of U.S. involvement in the war, Clark was often overwhelmed at these events. At another volatile debate, a young Communist sympathizer stormed up to him and said, "You are killing our comrades in Vietnam. Now we will kill you." According to a *New York Times* reporter, "there might have been a knife brandished." Clark was shaken: "I looked at his face and I knew it wasn't a joke. I felt my ears start to burn." The man was dragged away, but the Clarks did not sleep well that night.[10]

"He had a tremendous sense of loyalty to the army and a tremendous sense of duty that the official story was well told and well advocated," said Early. "Some of the Americans disagreed with his position, but understood why he felt compelled to be an advocate of American policy in Vietnam. They would respect him for that, but not necessarily agree with him."[11]

Clark was also stung by the anti-American sentiment he found in some churches. "When I went to Protestant services in England," he said, "there was a tremendous passion against America's [involvement] in Vietnam. It became personal against the men in the armed services. It wasn't just the policy. It was the people. To me, that wasn't an atmosphere in which I felt comfortable." Clark had attended Catholic Mass several times with Gert when they were dating because she did not want to go to Protestant services. "In those days, Catholics were much less ecumenical than they are today," said Clark. (Gert softened her view on this over the years and became comfortable attending Protestant services.) When Clark began to go to Catholic Mass with Gert, he was attracted to its "reasoned, structured, ordered consistency."[12]

The more he attended mass, the more he found a refuge in the Catholic Church. "I wouldn't have known anything about Catholicism if I hadn't been dating Gert," he said. "I had tried to go to the Protestant churches in England, and I had sought out a Baptist church and a Methodist church. In both cases the sermons were against the American military and full of wildly overstated claims about how bad the American military was. When I saw and felt this animus out of these Protestant churches in England during the Vietnam War, it just turned me off."[13]

Clark's interest in Catholicism was nurtured at Oxford when he met a Catholic priest and World War II veteran named Michael Hollings. "He was from one of the original Catholic families who had disobeyed Henry VIII's order to renounce the Roman Catholic faith," Clark said. "And he was just an incredibly educated, literate, bright, insightful, experienced man—a real leader. . . . We went to some youth groups and various student groups and I determined I would convert to Catholicism based on his witness, but never had time to do it."[14]

Vietnam was never far from Clark's mind at Oxford. "He knew where he was headed," said Early. "He had friends in Vietnam already, some of his friends from West Point were being shot at, if not killed, and that was pretty tough stuff."[15] One of those friends was Arthur M. Parker III, who had been Clark's roommate during his senior year at the academy. Atkinson related the story in *The Long Gray Line:* "He was struck by a helicopter rotor blade near Hué while pushing his men to safety. For four days Parker lay on the hospital ship U.S.S. *Sanctuary* before dying. He left behind a widow and seven-month-old son."[16]

Clark and Hottell spent many long nights talking about Vietnam. "After we stayed up late one night discussing life and death and Vietnam, we finally came back to the adage, 'If there's nothing worth fighting and dying for, then there's nothing worth living for,'" said Clark.[17] When Hottell received his orders for Vietnam, he used those same words in the obituary he wrote for his family to use in case he died. He was killed in a helicopter crash in 1970.

Back home in Little Rock, Veneta Clark received a call one day from one of the Kanne relatives, Molly Friedman, who lived in England. She asked Veneta for permission to call Wesley at Oxford, introduce herself as his cousin, and tell him about his Jewish ancestry. Veneta agreed; her son was now twenty-three years old and she had kept the truth from him long enough. Friedman called Clark's apartment during the day, when Clark was studying at school, and spoke to Gert. When Clark got home, Gert gave him the news. "You got a call from this Molly Friedman, who says she's your cousin." They talked about the surprising call, and Gert asked Clark if he had ever heard anything about Jewish roots in his family. "I wasn't aware of any, but maybe," Clark said.[18]

Clark called his cousin back and they soon met. She told him the whole story—the Russian immigrants, the weekly Sabbaths at his grandparents' house, his father's attendance at the KAM Temple, his mother's desire to protect him from prejudice. Clark called his friend and former West Point roommate, Theodore Hill, to share the news and help him process it. "He was in shock," recalled Hill. "He asked me how I would feel. I told him it was a spectacular, positive thing. I think he was quiet. I think he agreed. He was just realizing how much he had learned just from that one piece of information."[19]

Clark didn't discuss the news with his mother until he returned to the States. "When I went home I confronted her and I asked her, 'Mom, you never told me. Why? ... I don't understand why you didn't tell me.' She started to cry. She said, 'Wesley, you just had enough problems. You didn't need one more. You'd lost your father. You came down to Little Rock. You were in fights a lot. You had a Chicago accent. You just didn't need one more problem.'"[20]

Once he learned about it at Oxford, he didn't try to hide it. "I was interested to find out about it," he said. "I was actually thrilled to be able to complete the family history. Of course, while I was a young man I'd read the book *Exodus* and seen the movie and studied Israeli military actions: the War of Independence, the 1956 war. They were incredibly bold and daring military forces. I was proud."[21]

Clark's Jewish ancestry was reported during his campaign for the Democratic presidential nomination in 2003, but he corrected reporters who made it appear that it was a recent discovery in his life (as it had been for Madeleine Albright when she learned about her Jewish roots only after she became secretary of state). "It was well acknowledged over time," he told the Associated Press that October. "There was no sudden discovery."[22]

Clark's academic performance at Oxford was excellent—his tutor assessed him as "one of the three best PPE men" in his college—and he nearly made First Honors. (The vast majority of students fell into the Second Honors category, which covered a wide ranking. Surprisingly, Bill Bradley, the future senator who had arrived at Oxford a year ahead of Clark, played so much basketball for the university that he only made Third Honors.) The official Army Academic Report, written by his tutor, details how close he came to making the prestigious First Honors at Magdalen College:

> He obtained very good second class honours indeed in Philosophy, Politics, and Economics, his marks on five papers out of eight being on the margin of the first and second class, which resulted in his being given a *viva voce* examination for first class honours, in which he failed by a small margin to improve on his written performance. He must have been in the top 15 percent of the entire university, and was certainly one of the three best PPE men in this college.
>
> His performance was particularly impressive because he came within an ace of being the first West Point man at Oxford (I think) to get a First in PPE in two years rather than three. His marks on four economics papers were particularly impressive, but he showed himself an all-rounder by reaching the margin of the first class also in government and general philosophy. He would certainly be a considerable asset in the Social Studies department at the Academy. He is a man who not only works hard but goes deep and thinks clearly. He is not so much a natural intellectual as a man who demands the maximum from himself, and is never satisfied to rest on a routine performance. He would make, I think, not a loquacious but a stimulating teacher.[23]

Clark has always remained in touch with his Oxford

colleagues, including Early and their British friend, Robin Janvrin, who is now personal secretary to Queen Elizabeth and runs all her affairs. When Clark and Early get together, the first thing they do is "go to the swimming pool to see who's fittest."[24]

As he would learn throughout his career in the army, Clark's Rhodes scholarship came with a price. "Wes was always looked on as too well educated, too wired, too good-looking," said one of Clark's friends, retired U.S. Army Gen. Barry McCaffrey. "He's not a simple crunch soldier. The Rhodes scholars have always been a little suspect in the army."[25] Clark had already learned at West Point that high achievement garnered resentment from some quarters. "In the United States Army, from the time I was a West Point captain, really, I was sort of a marked man," he said. "There are three terrible things that can happen to you in the United States Army, if you're an officer. You can win a congressional Medal of Honor. You can be a Heisman Trophy winner. Or you can be a Rhodes scholar."[26]

After leaving England in the summer of 1968, the Clarks spent three months at Fort Knox, Kentucky, where the young lieutenant went through the Armor Officer Basic Course. His training included classroom study of tank weaponry and maintenance as well as realistic field exercises. He learned every nut and bolt of the M48 Patton, the "jungle-buster" tank used in Vietnam to plow tracks through dense vegetation and attack Viet Cong bunkers. The four-crew, 52-ton tank's gunnery included a 90 mm cannon and two machine guns. Cyclone fencing was often set up around the tanks when they were stationery to protect them from the enemy's rocket-propelled grenades.

Clark finished the course as a "Distinguished Graduate" and immediately went on to Fort Benning, Georgia, to take the Ranger Course. The training was covered in three parts: hand-to-hand combat and other maneuvers at Fort Benning, mountain tactics and survival in north Georgia, and jungle training in the Florida panhandle. "Ranger training was the first hurdle in the army," Atkinson wrote, "and it would fell nearly a third of them in under six months. . . . Ranger was intended to build soldiers—tough, indomitable soldiers, who were hard physically and harder psychologically." Beneath the bland, official description of the course, "lay another, implicit purpose . . . to keep men alive in Vietnam."[27] The jungle training was the most brutal, designed to re-create the stress and confusion of real battle. Trainees routinely suffered from exhaustion, malnutrition, snakebites, scorpion stings, spider bites, and twisted joints. The instructors were carefully selected Vietnam combat veterans who incorporated what they had learned in battle into the training.

Clark's military report stated his "performance throughout the course was outstanding. He demonstrated in and out of leadership positions his natural ability to work with men and effectively lead them. His drive, motivation, and physical stamina were exemplary—often encouraging slower students to more satisfactory performance. He displayed excellent military bearing and presence."

Clark was promoted to captain, and his first assignment as an armor officer was as the commander of A Company, Fourth Battalion, Sixty-eighth Armor, Eighty-second Airborne Division at Fort Riley, Kansas. His five-month command of this light tank company was highlighted by the high rating his company made for a major inspection that occurred while they were fully occupied in supporting a complex infantry exercise. They had three hours to prepare for the inspection, and Clark's superiors were impressed with their performance. "Upon his assumption of command he immediately took positive action to improve the supply, maintenance, administrative, and training posture of Company A," wrote his commanding officer on his evaluation report. "The results were apparent in the fine showing Company A made during the Fifth Army Command Maintenance Management Inspection."

This first command proved that Clark's natural leadership and ability to motivate others—qualities that first appeared when he was a camp counselor and high school swim coach—translated well into his military career. His commanding officer remarked on a report that "the morale, enthusiasm, and general attitude of the company was so outstanding that it was favorably commented on by a large number of senior officers. This was largely due to the superior leadership of Captain Clark. Not content to only strive for high standards of performance, he also always considered first the welfare of the men under his command. The high esteem the men of Company A have for him is very evident." The comments of another officer on Clark's report were just as glowing and, as time would tell, prophetic. "Clark's rare combination of great intelligence and education coupled with the drive, organizational ability, and attention to detail of an outstanding troop leader should carry him to the highest positions with the U.S. Army."

With armor and ranger training and a first command behind him, Clark finally received his orders for duty in Vietnam. On May 21, 1969, he flew out from San Francisco to report to the First Infantry Division at Lai

Khe to work for the deputy chief of staff. His position, called the Assistant G3, was to support the deputies who ran the operations and planning of the staff. (In the general staff system, the G1 handles personnel; G2, intelligence; G4, logistics; G5, civil affairs.) His superior, Maj. Charles Toftoy, the Deputy G3, reported to the First Infantry Division's chief of staff, Col. A. G. Hume. For nearly eight months, Clark analyzed data, gave briefings to the commanding general, took on special research projects, and produced studies on military operations that, according to remarks in his military record, addressed "the effectiveness of ambushes, reallocation of air assets, the formation of a target destruction center," and others. Many of these studies were not assigned but formed on his own. He created analytical tools to evaluate the effectiveness of combat operations, which were put into practice at higher levels of the staff. These included a method for determining the time of day for peak enemy activity, and another to calculate "friendly troop density" compared to "the number of enemy contacts in the same area." His skill in devising studies and writing them up clearly got him reassigned as the G3 research and evaluation officer, a position normally filled by a major.

Clark was awarded the Bronze Star for his work on the staff. In evaluation reports, Maj. Toftoy called Clark "the best officer I have known based on his experiences and time in grade. I recommend that he be promoted ahead of his contemporaries. . . . The results of some of [his] studies have had an effect on the overall strategy of the Division." Another superior, Lt. Col. Frederic Brown, declared Clark "the most impressive young officer I have observed in thirteen years service. He is extraordinarily competent, wholly dedicated, and possesses a uniquely creative mind. I have used him as a Special Projects

Officer—assigned only the most difficult problems.... In each of these areas, he has produced original, innovative solutions. . . . He is without any doubt, general officer material. His career should be closely watched."

In January 1970 Clark's staff job was over; he received an infantry command and went into combat. He was made Commanding Officer, A Company, First Battalion, Sixteenth Infantry of the First Infantry Division. Just over one month in his command, Clark was leading a twenty-five-man platoon on a patrol when an enemy sniper shot him. In the confusion and split-second mayhem that his instructors had tried to replicate in ranger training, he first thought the buzzing around his head was a swarm of hornets. He tells the story in *Waging Modern War*:

> We were on patrol in the jungle, moving on foot in platoon strength, searching for the Viet Cong. . . . Our force found a small group in an old bunker complex—the buzzing around my head wasn't hornets but AK-47 rounds whizzing by, the dark stains on my leg and shoulder weren't perspiration but blood, and there was a white bone sticking out from my right hand as I looked down to see why I had dropped my rifle. I [directed] . . . one small element from our force of twenty-five to lay down a "base of fire" while another element maneuvered against the base camp from the flank."[28]

In a magazine interview, he provided more details of the attack: "The guy emptied an AK magazine at me, and I turned just as he fired, so he stitched me up the right side of my body instead of taking me in the throat and gut. He shot the M-16 out of my hand and put a hole in my leg and another one through my shoulder. I was lying on the ground bleeding and yelling [to my men], 'Get on your feet and assault now.'"[29]

When Michael McClintic saw his captain staggering, he ran to his side and pushed him down, out of the line of fire. Clark recalled shouting orders from the ground as he watched the soldier above him fire at the enemy and get hit by an AK-47 round. "The guy was actually there firing back while I was hollering at the company to come up," Clark said.[30] He and McClintic were the only two wounded during the ambush. The Viet Cong retreated, the platoon called in for evacuation support, and a helicopter arrived within minutes to airlift the two wounded to a hospital.

Clark recalled his first conversation with the staff: "When I got back, the doctor said, 'You got the million-dollar wound.' But I said, 'No!' I thought the million-dollar wound was when you lost your you-know-what."[31] What he had was an injury serious enough to take him out of combat, but not life-threatening. McClintic's wounds were less severe, and he would recover more quickly. Clark did not know McClintic's identity until thirty-three years later, when a *Boston Globe* reporter tracked McClintic down while researching a profile of Clark.

On February 21st, Clark's wife and parents heard the news via telegram:

THE SECRETARY OF THE ARMY HAS ASKED ME TO INFORM YOU THAT CAP-TAIN WESLEY K. CLARK WAS WOUNDED IN ACTION IN VIETNAM ON 19 FEBRUARY 1970. HE RECEIVED GUNSHOT WOUNDS TO THE RIGHT SHOULDER, RIGHT HAND WITH A FRACTURE OF THE SECOND METACARPAL; RIGHT HIP AND RIGHT LEG WITH A FRACTURE OF THE RIGHT FIBU-LAR WHILE ON A COMBAT OPERATION

WHEN A HOSTILE FORCE WAS ENCOUNTERED....

The next day they learned that he had been transferred to a hospital in Japan, and on March 2, they were told he was in satisfactory condition "and his prognosis is good." A few days later he was returned to the United States to recuperate for two months at Valley Forge General Hospital in Phoenixville, Pennsylvania.

When Clark left for Vietnam, Gert was three months pregnant. He didn't meet his son Wesley Jr. until he arrived at the hospital. "I saw him for the first time when he was four or five months old," he said. "I had a hook on my hand, and it scared her when I tried to hold him. He didn't seem to mind."[32] Throughout his tour of duty, he had kept a keepsake from Gert close to his heart, wearing the St. Michael medal she mailed him on his dog tags. He also found time to convert to Catholicism, which he had wanted to do since he graduated from West Point. "It wasn't until I got to Vietnam that I got to a Catholic priest in division headquarters and asked him if he could help me convert," he said. "He put me through a very simplified course."

Clark's faith didn't waver, even while patrolling swamps for a hidden enemy in a war where 66 percent of the casualties were in infantry. "I didn't have any doubts in Vietnam," he said. He took out his beads and prayed the rosary every day, reciting the "Hail Mary" he had memorized during his conversion process.[33] "I liked the long tradition of learning and study," he said of the Catholic Church. "I felt it served as more of an anchor, and I thought at this point that it was very important to be grounded in history. The prosaic thing to say is that of course religion is very important to a fighting man because there is no atheism in the foxhole. But there is actually a lot of truth to that. I don't think you can operate in this world unless you believe there is something more than just hedonism."[34]

After he was wounded, Clark had a spiritual experience that made him feel even more secure in his faith. He had just attended a church service near the hospital in Japan when he was overcome with a flood of religious feeling. "I remember coming out of that church and feeling like I had been—at that point I just felt very, very close to God and that I'd done the right thing with my life."[35]

Before his wounds took him out of his command, Clark had served his company well and received more outstanding reviews from his superior officers. "Captain Clark is an aggressive, intelligent officer who has commanded a mechanized infantry company in combat in a truly outstanding manner," wrote Lt. Col. David Martin. "His company had the reputation of being an aggressive, smooth functioning, fighting organization, which is a result of his exemplary leadership ability.... The stress of sustained combat operations has had no effect on him or the manner in which he responds." In summary, Martin described Clark as "an officer of unlimited potential, respected by his superiors, contemporaries, and subordinates." He recommended that Clark be promoted ahead of his contemporaries and "assigned to a function where his full potential can be realized."

Like all wounded soldiers, he was awarded the Purple Heart. He also received the Silver Star, the third highest military award, for heroism in combat. The citation read, in part: "Although painfully wounded in the initial volley, Captain Clark immediately directed his men on a counter-assault of the enemy positions. With complete disregard for his personal safety, Captain Clark remained with his unit until the reactionary force arrived and the situation was well in hand. His ... unquestionable valor in close combat against a hostile force is in keeping with the finest traditions of the military service."

McClintic received the Bronze Star for Valor "for acts of heroism performed in ground combat." Clark, recalling the soldier's acts decades later, remarked that McClintic "should have gotten something more . . . these awards were never fair."[36]

Clark was determined not to be classified as disabled and subsequently furloughed out of the army. He had lost muscle tissue from his right thumb, and in spite of one-quarter of missing flesh from his right calf, he refused to accept the prognosis that he would never walk without a limp. He overcame his injuries over twelve months of rehabilitation therapy and trained himself back to top physical shape—in upcoming army physical fitness tests, taken throughout his career, he sometimes received perfect scores.

At West Point, Clark had learned that his job was to win America's wars. He knew what he was getting into in Vietnam, and he was not surprised by his experiences there. "I'd done a lot of studying and a lot of thinking about it going in," he said. "What I saw there wasn't any different from my expectations. I wasn't angry. I liked the army. I'd been treated well. I was part of the team. . . . I think when you are wounded and you shed blood for your country, it binds you to it in a way nothing else can."[37]

FIVE

★ ★ ★ ★

In Command

"For the U.S. Army, [the collapse of the Soviet Union] was also a time of enormous change because we lost our yardstick. Year in and year out we could gauge the relentless growth of Soviet military power as it poured out new weapons . . . against which we could measure ourselves. . . . All these measurements were gone by 1991. . . . We had to begin a new way of looking at the armed forces and the army."
—Wesley Clark[1]

"It is simply not possible to overstate the significance of Col. Wes Clark's impact on our army."
—Brigadier General Edwin Leland[2]

Company C of the Thirty-second Armor Division was a small, hobbling group of wounded men when Clark became their commander at Fort Knox, Kentucky, in 1970. Like them, Clark was recovering from his war injuries, unable to do routine physical exercise or shoot a gun. His mission was to lead the seventy-man company in providing light tanks for the base's armor school. Company C was 60 percent understaffed, but the demands placed on it by the school had not diminished.

Clark has fond memories of this command and is proud of what his men accomplished under such difficult circumstances. "I found a group of people in the army I loved," he told an audience in Little Rock in 2001. "Everybody in the company had been wounded.... The [soldier] who looked after weapons couldn't walk; he was on crutches. Other people couldn't use their hands. I had a hand and a leg wound. I couldn't run or do PT [physical training] or shoot a pistol or anything. But somehow, we all hung together, we worked ninety days straight that summer."

All of his men were draftees, but "they'd all served their country, they'd given their blood, and they were proud to have served their country." Reenlistments were very rare during the war, but his company won the battalion reenlistment award that summer because they reenlisted *one* soldier to stay in the army. "It was a tough time," said Clark, "but I love those men, and that's why I stayed with it. And over the years we built the United States Army and our nation's military back up in strength."[3]

Company C helped Clark realize why he wanted to make the army his lifetime career. "They were good people, and I loved that company more than any other command I ever had because of what the soldiers meant to me," he said in 1997. "That convinced me more than anything else to stay in the army because I loved the experience of working with the troops."[4] His mandated four-year commitment to the army would be up in 1971, soon after he left Company C, but by then Clark knew that he wanted to continue his military career and stick with his West Point goal of becoming a general one day.

In his first book, Clark reflected on his feelings as a soldier during an unpopular war and on the challenge the army faced in the following decades. "Bullet wounds, I learned, healed in a few months, but the emotional isolation from our contemporaries, the sense of rejection that we felt, and the lack of public appreciation lingered. . . . Like other military men of my generation, I spent much of my military career helping to rebuild the war-shattered U.S. Army and to learn and embed in it the lessons to prevent another disaster like Vietnam."[5]

Clark's West Point classmate Robert H. Scales, a U.S. Army general and historian, described the state of the army after the war in one of his books on military history:

> The American Army emerged from Vietnam cloaked in anguish. In the early seventies it was an institution fighting merely to maintain its existence in the midst of growing apathy, decay, and intolerance. Forty percent of the army in Europe confessed to drug use, mostly hashish; a significant minority, 7 percent, was hooked on heroin. . . . Barracks became battlegrounds between blacks and whites. Racial violence spread into the streets of garrison communities from Fayetteville, North Carolina, to Bamberg, Germany.[6]

Like the ailing but strong-willed C Company, the army did rebuild and became part of an overhauled military that proved itself in Kosovo and Desert Storm. And Clark, committed to a year of painful physical therapy to regain his strength and flexibility, also succeeded, despite his doctor's bleak prognoses. Proof of this came not only through his continued promotions and commands, but also in his performance in the army's semiannual Physical Readiness Tests. In 1983, for example, he received a Certificate of Achievement for making "a maximum evaluation score" on the test, which was "highly indicative of your physical readiness to perform all assigned tasks."

At Fort Knox, Clark also worked as president of the Brigade Junior Officer Council, teaching junior officers how to become more professional in their methods. His evaluation reports reflect the positive effect he had on his men and how well his understaffed company performed. "In spite of long duty hours, his company's morale rose constantly," wrote Lt. Col. Thomas Woodley. "His experience in dealing with soldiers, his ingenuity in finding unusual solutions to management problems, his personal magnetism and his dedication to . . . the soldiers' welfare produced spectacular results." Col. Harry Smythe reported that "Clark's performance was the best of 35 unit commanders in the brigade during this period. . . . [He] has the rare combination of intelligence, dedication, and leadership ability which indicates a potential for the highest levels of responsibility."

Traditionally, many officer evaluations are inflated with praise, sometimes to the point that it is difficult to distinguish between the outstanding and merely good. But in most cases, Clark was singled out as a top man throughout his career and, in spite of the exaggerated style of the reports, stood out among his peers.

Clark stayed at Fort Knox for the next eight months, continuing his officer training in the Armor Officer Advanced Course. He took two additional courses as electives, in national security management and nuclear & chemical target analysis, and wrote an article that won the Armor Association Writing Award. Clark also "actively participated in community affairs" during the course, all "while breezing through the Advance Course, leading his class by a wide margin," according to his faculty adviser,

Lt. Col. Arthur Stebbins. He skipped the twenty-hour review provided for the final exam in the target analysis class, and still received the highest marks.

Clark left Fort Knox in the spring of 1971 to take a short-term staff position in Washington, DC, working in the Office of the Chief of Staff as special assistant for the Modern Volunteer Army. Now a twenty-six-year-old captain, Clark's spent two months designing a new education program for enlisted men. His proposal was adopted as army policy, one part of the new effort to create a modernized all-volunteer force. Brig. Gen. Robert Montague wrote Clark up as "one of the best captains I have ever known," adding that he was "especially good at working with civilians." Another reviewer on Clark's record, Lt. Gen. George Forsythe, was impressed with the officer overall, and described him as a man with an "unusually high level of moral courage, integrity, and character."

In the summer of 1971, the Clarks moved to West Point where Clark began a three-year teaching assignment. Just five years after graduating from the academy himself, Clark was an instructor teaching principles of economics to a class of sixty cadets and coaching the debate team. In his first semester, the assistant professor who taught political philosophy was unexpectedly reassigned and Clark was asked to take over his class. In that class, he introduced cadets to the philosophy of American government and the moral and legal concerns that relate to it. His students studied the classic writings on the subject and discussed how they applied to current-day issues. Within a year, he was advanced to assistant professor, a move that occurred "only in extraordinary cases," according to his superior in the department of social sciences, Associate Professor Lt. Col. William Wix.

Clark had a talent for teaching, according to one of his

fellow social science instructors, Col. Jack Jacobs. "He was extremely knowledgeable, a very compelling teacher," Jacobs said, "and he was extremely well-liked by the students." Jacobs described their job at the academy as "absolutely glorious—you have an opportunity to have a profound effect on the intellectual ability of people who will be leaders of the army. You learn a great deal yourself, and it's nice dealing with these kids who go out and defend the republic."[7]

Clark and Jacobs also ran together for exercise, and Jacobs credits Clark for helping him get back into shape during their time together on the faculty. "Wes was instrumental in getting me back running," he said. "I had quit and was not in particularly good shape; I got out of the hospital in early 1973 and came to the military academy to teach a little earlier than anticipated." Jacobs had been in the hospital recovering from severe combat wounds; his actions in Vietnam had earned him the Congressional Medal of Honor, the nation's highest military award, as well as two Silver Stars and three Bronze Stars for his heroism on the battlefield. "Wes grabbed me one day and said let's go out and run, and he got me started running again," Jacobs said. "He was persistent and ran with me; he thought it was important that I get in good physical condition. I eventually ran marathons."[8]

The scenic Hudson River and rolling hills of Orange County made West Point a beautiful place to raise Wesley Jr. in his preschool years, and New York was a short train ride away for visits to his grandparents in Brooklyn. The Clarks lived in comfortable faculty housing on the academy grounds, and rarely would they be this close to Gert's family in the decades of military life that followed.

Clark's out-of-classroom time was also spent assistant coaching for the swim team, doing research, writing scholarly articles, and serving on committees. He taught platoon tactics during one summer training program, and continued to coach the debate team every semester. Clark thrived in this academic environment and was considered an exemplary teacher and coach. "Every program with which he has been associated has been singularly successful," wrote a superior. "The debate program has had its best record in intercollegiate in over ten years.... The Plebe [swimming] team is undefeated and the A Squad has a 5-1 record." Col. Lee Olvey, chairman of the social sciences department, also commended Clark on the results he achieved in the debate program: "Your knowledge of debate technique and strategy has enabled cadets to accomplish constant improvement, eventually resulting in one of the most successful seasons of the last decade." Academy Superintendent William Knowlton often asked Clark to serve on committees dealing with school policy, and Olvey remarked, "I have not known an officer as junior as he whose counsel has been so widely sought. . . . Clark has a brilliant mind and inexhaustible energy for work and concern for the army as an institution that is unique among officers of his age and grade. He has the finest qualities of character and personality and commands the highest respect from subordinates and superiors."

Associate Professor Lt. Col. William Taylor made additional comments about Clark's character on a performance review: "Twice during the rating period, Captain Clark has refused to take credit for his own significant accomplishments. On both occasions, he insisted that another officer, not he, was deserving of praise."

In one particularly florid review, Col. George Osborn described Clark as "generally quiet and reserved, but has an excellent sense of humor and almost unfailingly cheerful. He has mastered the Socratic discourse as a technique of teaching, and he uses it with outstanding effect in the classroom. In an old-fashioned sense, this man is a teacher whose students love him, i.e., they respect and almost revere him because they know he has something important to tell them about the important issues that have plagued men for time immemorial."

Daniel Christman, who had graduated first in the class of 1965 at West Point, taught with Clark in the same department, and saw firsthand how popular Clark was with the students. "He was clearly someone who identified with the young cadet and vice versa," he said. "The beauty of the West Point faculty model is to bring back people like Clark who had just come from a combat tour, who were older than the cadets but not much, and who shared a lot of their interests because they weren't separated by generations."[9]

In addition to the age and combat experience factors, Christman identified the personal characteristics that made Clark an especially effective teacher at the academy. "He had a particular magic because of his energy and his clear intellect," he said, adding that Clark's work as a debate coach and leader in other extracurriculars helped him identify more closely with the cadets as well. "He was able to relate what was going on in cadet and student life with what was going in the classroom," said Christman. Those things made him a popular professor. You wouldn't think students would flock to a class like political philosophy, but they wanted to get into it because it was taught by Clark. The story was, 'You've got to get in, meet this young captain, take his course—you'll love it.'"[10]

Clark's three highly productive years at the academy were recognized with the Army Commendation Medal.

The citation described him as an "exceptional teacher," a debate coach "largely responsible for the best three-year record in intercollegiate debate competition at the Military Academy," and an officer who "exemplified self-less devotion to the Corps of Cadets."

On one of Clark's performance reviews at West Point, Taylor recommended that he be selected to attend the Command and General Staff College (CGSC) and promoted to major "at the first opportunity." The army followed that recommendation, and Clark left for the military graduate school at Fort Leavenworth after the 1974 spring term. He enrolled in the Command and General Staff Officer Course, a ten-month program to train captains and majors for higher levels of command. The course required a master's thesis, and Clark did a study of the Rolling Thunder air campaign in Vietnam entitled "Military Contingency Operations: The Lessons of Political–Military Coordination." This study dealt with the failure of America's policy of "gradualism," in which strikes were designed by political decision in Washington rather than by military planners in the middle of the action.

"I reviewed as much as I could find about Vietnam, reread the Pentagon Papers, and researched the problem of contingency operations," wrote Clark. "To successfully 'compel,' I realized, the force applied must be much greater than we had been willing to commit at the time, must be intensified more rapidly, and must be directed at achieving significant military ends."[11] In his thesis, Clark wrote, "Once committed to actual combat, anything less than overwhelming and rapid military success for the intervening power will be diplomatically disastrous."[12] This theory of applying strong and sudden force was also developed by other officers in the post-Vietnam era and would later come to be known as the "Powell Doctrine."

In June 1975, Clark graduated at the top of his class at CGSC, received his second master's degree (master of military arts and science), and was promoted to major. This distinction helped him win a prestigious appointment as a White House Fellow, and he moved his family to Washington, DC, that summer. Before his fellowship began in August, Clark worked for a few weeks in the Army Personnel Center, helping launch a long-term study.

The White House Fellows Program is extremely competitive: out of 2,307 applicants in 1975, only fourteen were chosen.[13] Clark went through a lengthy selection process including regional and national finals and a series of personal interviews in Washington, DC. Then, as now, the selection commission looked for gifted, highly motivated young people who had already made extraordinary achievements in their professions and shown a commitment to public service. The program's mission is to give future leaders working knowledge of government that they will utilize throughout their careers, whether in government, the military, or the private sector. Fellows get firsthand experience in federal government, serving as full-time, paid special assistants to cabinet-level officials. In addition, the educational aspect of the fellowship includes travel abroad and seminars with government officials including Supreme Court justices, senior White House staff, the vice president and cabinet secretaries, and corporate leaders as well. Colin Powell had recently been a fellow in 1972–1973, and Clark's group included Dennis Blair, a navy officer who would lead the Pacific Command from 1999 to 2002.

Clark was assigned to the Office of Management and Budget (OMB), and worked as special assistant to the director, James T. Lynn. President Gerald Ford had recently appointed Lynn to the post; prior to this he had been secretary of housing and urban development. The Ford administration faced several historical challenges during Clark's fellowship period of August 1975 to August 1976. The office of the presidency had been eroded by the Watergate scandal, and President Ford took the oath of office in August 1974 stating, "Our long national nightmare is over." The United States and the Soviet Union were deep into the Cold War, each holding massive nuclear arsenals and contributing to global anxiety about nuclear annihilation. The Paris peace talks of 1973 had officially ended U.S. involvement in Vietnam, but failed to end the fighting. Four months before Clark started his fellowship, South Vietnam collapsed and U.S. Marines and Air Force helicopters conducted a massive airlift to fly American civilians and South Vietnamese refugees out of Saigon. Television pictures of that evacuation were seared in everyone's memory.

Lynn gave his special assistant several projects at the OMB. For three months, Clark worked six days a week preparing a report on budget issues that was published as part of the President's Fiscal Year 1977 Budget. He directed a departmental task force to analyze overhead and administrative costs in government and to recommend procedures to reduce costs, and participated in another task force that studied military compensation. Lynn also gave him a six-week special assignment to serve as special assistant to John Marsh, counselor to the president. Clark helped Marsh write a review that advised President Ford about changes in the structure of the intelligence community. In addition to foreign educational travel with the entire fellows group, Clark traveled extensively with Lynn, including trips to Israel and other parts of the Middle East. During the visit to Israel, Clark got a close look at the Israeli military and was very impressed. "They have a national passion for bold military solutions," he said after returning from the trip. "In every case, they are beautiful tacticians, daring, courageous, and very, very skillful. As a military professional, I have the greatest admiration for the skill of the Israeli military."[14]

That trip was especially moving for Clark, who for the past approximately eight years had been learning more about his Jewish ancestry. The tidbits of Israeli history that he had read about in his childhood held more meaning for him now, and he was pleased to know that he was connected to the warriors he met in Israel. "I was proud," he said, adding that he had always admired the Israeli military. "While I was a young man, I'd read the book *Exodus* and seen the movie and studied Israeli military actions: The War of Independence, the 1956 war . . . and the 1967 war. They were incredibly bold and daring military forces."[15]

During his post as a White House Fellow, Clark was interviewed by the *Arkansas Democrat-Gazette* about his duties and travels. The reporter reminded him about a comment he had made back in his cadet days about wanting to "be a general one day." Clark, now thirty-one, modified his goal—somewhat. He said that he wanted "to contribute and make this country a better place to live," but added, "although you can contribute at every rank, naturally one likes to have more responsibility."[16] Clark's work over the year impressed the director, who wrote in a performance letter, "Major Clark is the most able White House Fellow I have known during my seven years in Washington."

In the spring of 1976, during his stint as a White House Fellow, Clark met up with his friend and classmate John "Jack" Wheeler, who asked him and another classmate, Matt Harrison, if they would be interested in helping him create a Vietnam memorial at West Point. Wheeler wanted to create something dedicated to all who had served, not just cadets or other army personnel. He went to Clark "because of Wes's instinct for what matters and for committing himself."[17] It would be the beginning of a long association on this project as well as in working out Wheeler's next project of building a national Vietnam Veterans' Memorial in Washington, DC.

"To raise that kind of idea in 1976 was just off the rails as far as a lot of people were concerned; technically, the war had only been over for one year and it was too close to the event," said Wheeler. "But the memory of those killed in action was a searing memory for all of us." They succeeded in building the memorial at West Point, and over the next few years Clark played a major role in helping raise the $10 million for the national monument. "He lent his considerable prestige and put his shoulder to the wheel," said Wheeler. "I could not have walked down that road without him."[18]

Wheeler knew that getting congressional approval for a national monument designated to an unpopular war and finding a location and design upon which everyone could agree was going to be a challenge of mythic proportions. He also knew that Clark cared enough about the soldiers' memories to take on such a challenge without a second thought. "He was a blood member of the class fellowship," said Wheeler. "He was a leader who took risks. I knew that without asking him.[19] In *The Long Gray Line*, Atkinson devotes many pages to the saga of building the memorial, which was completed in 1982 and dedicated on Veterans Day of that year. Etched into its black stone panels are the names of 57,939 dead, creating a wall, Atkinson writes, that became "a threshold where the dead also met the living."[20]

At the end of his White House fellowship, Clark moved with his family to Bamberg, Germany, where he took over the operations and training program for U.S. Army Europe's Thirty-fifth Armor unit. As an S3 officer in peacetime, Clark was responsible for improving the 569-man tank battalion's skills and efficiency to make them combat-ready. He created new methods for the division's tank operations, such as a new techniques for maintaining tanks that "greatly enhanced equipment reliability and performance," according to one superior. Clark devised new exercises, both written and hands-on, to help soldiers prepare for their evaluation tests, and managed all the technical training and other educational programs offered by the division. His achievements with this armor division were rewarded with a Meritorious Service Medal, and the comments on his officer evaluation reports reveal the respect he received from his commanding officers. Battalion Cmdr. Lt. Col. L. G. Nowak wrote:

> The most brilliant and gifted officer I've known.... Tough minded, forceful, yet sensitive to soldiers. Sets the highest standards, demands, and gets results. Upgraded individual, unit, and battalion training programs to best in Division as demonstrated on ARTEP Evaluation.... Excellent rapport

with Battalion officers who frequently sought his
advice on personal and professional matters. He
will be a superb battalion commander. Promote
him immediately.

And from Brig. Cmdr. Col. Charles Prather:

He was singularly outstanding, notably superb. The
battalion's operations improved continuously with
his guidance and leadership. Training became so
significantly better that word of Major Clark's
exceptional   talent   spread   throughout   the
division. . . . He is unquestionably one in a million. . . . I have never been more impressed with an
officer's talent and dedication. He should rank with
men like Douglas MacArthur, Maxwell Taylor, and
Creighton Abrams someday.

As Prather remarked, Clark's performance in the First
Armor spread throughout the division, and his accomplishments reached the desk of Gen. Alexander Haig, the
Supreme Allied Commander Europe (SACEUR). This
North Atlantic Treaty Organization (NATO) command,
headquartered in Belgium, was first held by General
Dwight Eisenhower upon the formation of NATO after
World War II. Haig chose Clark to join his staff as a special assistant. "The fact that General Haig selected him
for his personal staff is indicative of his caliber,"
remarked Brig. Gen. Clyde Spence Jr. an assistant division commander in Europe.

The SACEUR is simultaneously commander of all
U.S. forces in Europe, making this a two-channel command in which he reports to both the secretary general of
NATO and to the president of the United States (via the
secretary of defense and the chairman on the Joint Chiefs
of Staff). Accordingly, it is one of the most stressful and
complex commands in the military, and Clark came high-

ly recommended for Haig's staff as a brilliant thinker, analyst, and writer with a seemingly infinite capacity for work.

As Haig's special assistant, from February 1978 to June 1979, Clark's duties were diverse: He wrote the general's speeches, prepared policy reports and revised his defense plan, coordinated two multinational military exercises, and continued to create new methods for improving the army's combat readiness. Brigade Cmdr. Col. David Helela described Clark in this post as "creative, innovative, [and] bristling with initiative," and Brigade Executive Officer Lt. Col. Richard Schomberger wrote, "He has gained an enviable respect throughout the command." Maj. Gen. Robert Weitzel reported on Clark's total commitment to his superior officer and the job he represented, a characteristic that would also be recognized in his future posts: "Concerned self completely with needs of SACEUR and his subordinates at expense of personal welfare." Haig's remarks on Clark's evaluation report affirmed that Clark had lived up to the reputation he brought to the post:

> Major Clark is a totally outstanding officer. Poise, thoroughness, loyalty, brilliant insights, and a deep sense of professionalism and commitment to the army and Western security have been the hallmarks of his service. His unwavering sense of responsibility in all circumstances, thorough comprehension of complex issues, and unique sensitivity to the political and military realities of Allied security interests resulted in a level of performance and assignment of responsibilities normally reserved to general officers. Major Clark's career should continue to be monitored closely and upon completion of his command tour, he should be selected for attendance at the War College and assigned only to the most

responsible and demanding positions. Major Clark has clearly demonstrated a level of competence and motivation beyond his years and seniority—he is general officer material.

That glowing appraisal led to Clark's promotion to lieutenant colonel, and he was awarded the Legion of Merit medal for "exceptionally meritorious service in support of the North Atlantic Treaty Organization and Allied Command Europe." Sixteen months at Supreme Headquarters Allied Powers Europe (SHAPE) had offered Clark a working introduction to one of the world's largest commands. Unknown to him at the time, it was a warm-up to the day, eighteen years later, he would return to Belgium to take over the SACEUR command.

Clark's next post fit the pattern his career was forming. He described his role as similar to what the business community would call making "turnarounds" in low-performing areas. "I worked on coaching subordinates into achieving what they didn't dare dream," he explained.[21] From August 1979 to June 1982, Clark turned around an officer group and tank battalion at Fort Carson, Colorado. His first duty, as brigade executive officer, put him in charge of training the officers of the First Brigade, Fourth Infantry Division. This training included several aspects of command, from personnel management to intelligence to communications. His brigade commander, Col. Edwin Burba, stated that Clark "trained his staff officers to be professionals in every sense of the word. . . . Tempering brilliant intellect with pragmatic know-how and strong leadership qualities, Lt. Col. Clark is the most gifted officer of his rank in the army today."

After eight months working with the brigade officers, Clark was given command of the First Battalion's

Seventy-seventh Armor unit at Fort Carson. His mission was to produce where the outgoing battalion commander had failed. On his first visit to the motor pool, he saw that the tanks and other vehicles were inoperable, lying in broken heaps on the concrete, with troops nowhere to be found. He put his high-energy, morale-boosting tactics into gear, and "less than six weeks later we had met all standards in the reinspection," wrote Clark. "I gave a lot of pep talks, I made it a point personally to inspect the tanks, including a detailed technical inspection, and I met individually with the company commanders.... They had begun to believe in themselves. We went on to earn a reputation for the best maintenance in the division and became one of the top battalions with great esprit and morale, too." He defined the system that worked on this battalion as well as others:

> I had found a command pattern that worked: Be personally competent. Know and work the details; set high standards; provide lots of personal, up-front leadership and good planning; and work to bring out the best in the people you have. Make them achieve more than they ever thought possible, but never forget that they are also human beings. Look after the families, and deal with the whole person.[22]

The commander at Fort Carson, Gen. John Hudacheck, had a well-known aversion to West Point cadets and fast-risers like Clark. Even though Clark made quick and outstanding progress with the armor unit, Hudacheck expressed his attitude toward Clark by omitting him from a list of battalion commanders select-ed to greet a congressional delegation visiting the base. David Halberstam describes the incident in his book, *War in a Time of Peace: Bush, Clinton, and the Generals*:

"I'm afraid the old man [Hudacheck] doesn't consider you representative of the battalion commanders," one of the top staff officers told Clark. It was a
singular slap in the face; Clark had been judged as
somehow different, not one of the boys. His own
battalion's excellence—of that there was no
doubt—had made no difference. This was some
new kind of scoring that he could not fathom, based
not on performance, but instead on undefinable
qualities of personality.[23]

In Clark's first-year efficiency report, Hudacheck
gave him a mediocre "second block" grade, which at that
point in Clark's career could have been lethal to his
future in the army. Fort Carson was a crucial command,
and Hudacheck's lukewarm assessment could severely
limit his opportunities for other commands. Clark and
Hudacheck spent hours talking over the report, and
Hudacheck finally upgraded his assessment to "block
one." Clark received the grade he deserved, but not without having to fight for it.

Clark's other superiors gave him the glowing reviews
that had become typical of his career. Col. Lester
Bennett described Clark's results at Fort Carson as
"immediate and dramatic," adding that he "assumed
command of the worst combat maneuver battalion in the
brigade. . . . [and] in a period of only three months,
through dynamic and personal leadership by example, he
has transformed the battalion into the leader or contender
for top honors in the division."

Brigade Cmdr. Col. Robert Alsheimer was equally
impressed: "Every once in a while one is privileged to
encounter an officer so uniquely gifted that the over-
worked superlatives commonly utilized on evaluation
reports are inadequate to effectively describe his duty

performance. Lieutenant Colonel Clark is that officer. A brilliant, dynamic, and exceptionally innovative commander, his battalion has been characterized by superb esprit, discipline and professionalism throughout this entire rating period." In Clark's final evaluation of 1982, Alsheimer stated that "Clark is the best tank battalion commander I have observed in 25 years of service." After listing the outstanding performance of the armor battalion soldiers in their inspections and tests, he added that "the battalion has not had an AWOL or barracks theft in nearly a year, [and] achieved 223% of its reenlistment objective ... (tops in the Division). ... Clark's professionalism, dedication and outstanding leadership are worthy of the highest praise and clearly set him apart from his peers."

Another of Clark's superiors at Fort Carson, Brig. Gen. Colin Powell (who had experienced his own run-ins with Hudacheck), followed up Alsheimer's comments as follows: "The rater does not overstate. Wes Clark has been a superb battalion commander and will be a superb brigade commander. He is an officer of the rarest potential and will clearly rise to senior general officer rank. He will be one of the army's leaders in the 1990s."

In spite of his consistently outstanding success with both officers and the troops, Clark's experience with Hudacheck reemphasized that his educational background and speedy promotions were not in sync with the trends unfolding in the modernizing army. In 1981, in his first year at Fort Carson, Clark's name did not make the brigade command list. It was devastating news for an officer who had consistently risen to the top. "I slowly realized that I was going against the army tide of the time," he wrote, "which emphasized older commanders and deemphasized education and broadening experiences." He did not hide his disdain for the path he felt the army was taking:

> It was a time of the "country-boy" and "jes' plain soldierin'." Lots of people with fancy masters degrees and Ph.D.s kept it quiet if they could. It was the Vietnam backlash, though it took a long time to develop. I couldn't help what I had already done or how I had worked my way up. After the Rhodes scholarship and finishing at the top of the class in the Command and General Staff College, I had gotten an army-wide reputation, and I was stuck with it, for better or worse.[24]

Although the negative reaction to his career that he described did not show up on his evaluation reports, Clark knew he had detractors, as did other officers who had taken a similar route. This did not affect his commitment to the job, however. Clark lived out the "obsession of your public service" that MacArthur had demanded of the cadets at West Point.

In 1982, Clark learned that he had not made the brigade command list again, and he was so shaken that he considered leaving the army. "Others told him to stay the course," wrote Halberstam, "that even if he was having a hard time at Carson, there would be life after John Hudacheck."[25] His supporters were right; Clark survived his setback with Hudacheck and received a brigade command in 1986.

As he was out of the running for a command after his post at Fort Carson, Clark was selected to attend the military's most senior-level school, the National War College at Fort McNair in Washington, DC. This program focuses solely on national security and is designed to prepare both military and civilian professionals to analyze, write, and implement national security policy.

The college's location gave the students exposure to Washington leaders and many visiting diplomats and statespeople. Every morning, Clark and his 159 class-mates attended a lecture given by a guest speaker, often a U.S. or foreign government official. Clark's classes covered topics such as how the intelligence community and Congress impacted national security policy, the function of the National Security Council, strategies for using military force, the nature of power, and nonmilitary uses of power such as diplomacy and economics. One economics assignment, for example, required that students write up a complete federal budget. In the final weeks of the program, Clark put theory into practice in a group assignment called the "Crisis Decision Exercise," and he was selected to present his solution to the Terrorism Simulation exercise to the entire class. Clark's research paper, "Strategic and Doctrinal Implications of Deep Attack Concepts of the Defense of Central Europe," won first prize in the Chairman of the Joint Chiefs of Staff Group Strategy Essay Contest. In his spare time, Clark spent quality time in the college gym and played on the soccer, squash, and two-mile relay teams.

The National War College Commandant, Gen. Lee Surut, reported that Clark stood out from his classmates with a superior "grasp of European politico-military issues." Like many other evaluators during Clark's fif-teen-year career, Surut emphasized Clark's ability to challenge conventional wisdom and look at traditional problems from a new perspective. "By offering alternative solutions to difficult questions he encouraged others to think deeply and to consider alternatives as well," Surut wrote. "Clark has amply demonstrated all of the qualities necessary for success as a high-level commander or in planning, operations, policy, or strategy positions on the highest level joint of combined staffs. He is one of the most outstanding army officers I know and should be promoted well ahead of his contemporaries."

After receiving his diploma from the War College, Clark was promoted from lieutenant colonel to colonel. He stayed in Washington for another year to work at the Pentagon for Gen. Maxwell Thurman, the army's vice chief of staff. Thurman was one of the principal architects of the new army; as the head of the army recruiting command in 1979 he helped transform the army's image with his brainchild, the "Be all you can be" campaign. His aggressive and demanding style earned him the nickname "Mad Max," and according to one officer was known for "driving his staff crazy because he was a bachelor and the guy never went home."[26] Clark joined Thurman's staff in June 1983 as the chief of the army studies group.

Landing a staff position is, in the words of one of Clark's closest friends, Gen. Robert Scales, a time to pay one's dues to the Pentagon. Serving time on the administrative staff was mandatory for those who wanted to move ahead. Scales was at West Point with Clark, and like him had won a Silver Star for combat in Vietnam and pursued an academic route in the military, earning a Ph.D. in history from Duke University. Clark's job with the army studies group was to provide Thurman with new proposals on many aspects of the evolving modern army, from tactics and training to military strategy and research. "We both spent a lot of time writing and studying the issues," said Scales. "It was very high pressure work because of the nature of what we were doing. General Thurman was a very demanding sort of guy and put a lot of pressure on all of us to perform. It was a tough period for us all."[27]

Although the work was challenging and provided

them with an opportunity to work with the army's top leadership, it was still a staff job and medium-level officers looked forward to getting back into a command position. "Anytime you have a job like that, the first thing you try to do is get out of it," said Scales. "I know Wes wasn't particularly happy there; he had come from commanding a battalion. This was his time on the cross, it was his time to pay his dues at the Pentagon. And he was brilliant at it simply because of his ability to think through problems and arrive at quick solutions."[28]

In the fall of 1983 Clark took a few days away from the staff to attend a leadership program in France sponsored by the French-American Foundation. Also attending the foundation's Young Leaders Program that year was Hillary Rodham Clinton, wife of second-term Governor Bill Clinton and an attorney with the Rose Law Firm in Little Rock. It had been fifteen years since Clark had first met her future husband at Georgetown, and the relaxed style of the conference gave Clark and Hillary an opportunity to get acquainted and fill each other in on their careers.

Working for Thurman apparently gave Clark a new jolt of enthusiasm for the importance of training the new army, and he volunteered to bring his proven "turnaround" techniques to the National Training Center in California after his stint at the Pentagon. Thurman noted this move on Clark's evaluation, and recommended him for a promotion and future commands:

> Wes Clark was unknown to me before he reported to the Chief's Office as the leader of the Army Studies Group. Wes is a brilliant and dynamic organizer and leader. He quickly grasps concepts, develops the strategy for execution and can get most anything done with tact and energy. He is a

gifted visualizer who can make good things happen
in the Pentagon and in the field. Volunteered to go
to the National Training Center so he could contribute to that vital effort. Personable, tactful, ener-
getic, smart, and troopwise—select Wes Clark for
immediate command of an armored/mech brigade;
after one year promote to Brigadier General. He has
the requisite moral and leadership qualities to
assume flag rank responsibilities at the highest levels of government.

Clark's work was rewarded with his second Legion of
Merit award, which recognized that his "vision, leadership and initiative produced thought-provoking studies
and resolved important policy issues for the Chief of
Staff, Army." The citation added that Clark's input led to
improvements in the army's training systems as well as in
several other areas.

Clark had volunteered to implement some of the
those improvements at the relatively new National
Training Center (NTC) at Fort Irwin, which covers 1,000
square miles of the Mojave Desert in southeastern
California. Although this base had been used as a combat
training camp since the Korean War, the army did not
establish the large-scale, world-class NTC there until
1980. When Clark arrived in 1984, the program was still
being developed, with a mission to "provide tough, realistic, combined arms and services joint training." As commander of the operations group, Clark revised the overall
program to make the training resemble actual battle situ-
ations even more. The commanding general of the center,
Edwin Leland, described Clark as "the architect/imple-
menter of the world's most realistic and effective combat
training." For one and one-half years, from August 1984 to
January 1986, Clark upgraded the program, oversaw the

training of 50,000 soldiers, managed a group of nearly 600 operations officers, and supervised the operation of the NTC's $100 million instrumentation system and 200 tanks, trucks, and other vehicles.

Leland remarked that Clark's "capacity for work is unsurpassed in my experience—[he] routinely accomplishes in one day more than even his most talented contemporaries can handle in a week." He also commented on Clark's range of skills and his role in the ever-evolving army: "He can do it all—think, write, speak, organize, motivate, and lead. Assignments should be carefully managed to provide a range of professional experience which will make our army stronger as he becomes part of our senior leadership." Col. William Streeter stated that Clark was "admired and respected by his officers and soldiers," adding that "he has taken them far beyond their so-called normal abilities."

Streeter also noted that Clark and his wife "make an unbeatable team." Gert's commitment to the army has always been as strong as her husband's according to her friend, Diana Scales. "We always said the military got two for the price of one with them," she said. "They believed in the same things, she had just as much energy as he did. She was very involved, and she works just as hard as Wes does." Scales described the Clarks as a dynamic couple who combined their strengths in a total commitment to their family and to the army. "They're both type-A people, and usually type-A people can stress each other out," said Scales. "But they complement each other, they're so good for each other. Gert was strongly involved in programs to make better schools for military families and to care for the soldiers. She's also very bright and a quick study, like Wes."[29]

Wesley Jr. was fifteen years old when they arrived at

Fort Irwin. Like other military kids, he had grown accustomed to moving, changing schools, and making new friends every few years. He recalled that it was a big treat if the family went out to McDonald's once a month. His father admitted that "we were always on the road. It was a great standard of living, as long as you didn't value cash flow."[30] They lived paycheck to paycheck, and the year after they left this post, Clark spent a full month repairing an old car because he couldn't afford to buy another one. "We lived pretty close to the edge, even when I was an officer," Clark said.[31] But they were a close family; father and son read C. S. Lewis stories together, and during Clark's posts in Germany and Belgium he had taken Wes Jr. to museums and churches.

Gert was a partner in her husband's work to improve the quality of life of army soldiers and their families, and Wes Jr. observed this throughout his childhood. From base to base as they moved throughout the country, Gert served on Army Community Service and Red Cross boards. She realized how difficult it could be for young families to relocate often, and both she and her husband tried to help those transitions. "As a junior officer, a senior officer, you're responsible for other people, and you have to connect with them," she said. "It's not giving people orders; these are families, you have to connect. Particularly in the military community, it's very difficult changing duty stations every year or two, so helping people out and having them adjust to where they are is very important."[32]

Wes Jr. recalled the human factor of his father's mission while he was growing up. "They rebuilt the army in the 70s and 80s, not with M1 tanks and Apache helicopters; they rebuilt it by taking care of soldiers," he said.

"With affirmative action programs, with better housing, better healthcare, better education for the children."[33]

At the end of Clark's post as operations commander at NTC, Col. Carl Vuono rated him "an absolute superstar among a crowd of great colonels in our army." His revamping of the training program earned him another Meritorious Service Medal and Legion of Merit award. Not everyone was as impressed with Clark's performance as Vuono and the other raters, however. Gen. Dennis Reimer, who would cross paths with Clark again in his final two commands, considered him too hard on the senior officers who were underperforming at Fort Irwin. During a visit to the NTC, he "was reportedly unhappy, not with the results, but with the manner in which Clark operated," wrote Halberstam. "Other officers might have upgraded the program more slowly and with greater tact for the feelings of their peers. Not Clark. He drove it from the day he first arrived."[34]

Reimer's suspicions about Clark's tactics notwithstanding, in 1986 Clark received the brigade command he had been hoping for and left the NTC for Fort Carson, Colorado. In January he became brigade commander of two tank and one mechanized infantry battalions, leading 2,100 officers and soldiers. It was "an assignment I had long hoped to receive," he said.[35]

The Clarks enrolled Wes Jr. in the Fountain Valley School, a private high school on a 1,100-acre ranch in the foothills of the Rocky Mountains. The majestic setting of Fort Carson was a refreshing change from the desert base of Fort Irwin, California. In addition to the training and management responsibilities of his command, Clark continued to work on improving the lives of soldiers, which prompted one superior to report: "With equal vigor he attended to the quality of life issues of soldiers and family members." Gen. William Crouch observed that Clark was "absolutely brilliant, yet so disarmingly self-effacing, that he can lead anyone to excel. . . . People enjoy working for him because of his empathy as well as their success under his leadership."

Early in his command at Fort Carson, Clark's mother became ill with complications from a long history of high blood pressure. She and Victor had moved to Hot Springs, Arkansas, where they owned a house on Lake Hamilton. Veneta died on Mother's Day in May 1986, and the funeral was held back in Little Rock. She was buried at the Pine Crest Memorial Cemetery in Alexander, Arkansas, just outside of town. After her death, Victor moved back to Arkansas to live with his sister at the old family homestead in Paron. Jewel, who was by then a widow, had broken her hip and could not live on her own. Six years later, at age ninety, Victor underwent heart valve replacement surgery, from which he never recovered. After six months in intensive care, he died and was interred next to Veneta at Pine Crest.

After his command at Fort Carson, Clark was assigned to return to the Command and General Staff College at Fort Leavenworth, Kansas, this time to develop a senior officer–training program.

The Battle Command Training Program (BCTP) at the college was designed to teach senior officers how to command war. Clark refined the program for sixteen months, building it into "our army's premier means for training corps and division commanders in warfighting skills," according to Commanding Gen. William Mullen. His contribution was central to the upgrading of the army, as it provided for the first time an evaluation system for senior officers—one-, two-, and three-star generals. With an assessment program in place, these officers had a more clear-cut way to find out where they could improve and how.

"Imagine having a colonel who sets up a system to tell a two-star how well he was doing," remarked Lt. Gen. Dan Christman. "It's to Clark's great credit that the army gave him the responsibility to do it and that he could improve the commanders and staff that way, through that system."[36]

As he had done at the NTC, Clark made the training exercises more realistic. "Clark 'sold' the BCTP to the army; in turn, the field army has tested the BCTP and found that it exceeds expectations.... [Clark] is making a significant impact on army training," wrote Mullen. This successful command culminated in another promotion, one of the most significant of his career. Clark's teenage goal became a reality on November 1, 1989, when he received his first star as a brigadier general.

In July of that year he returned to the NTC at Fort Irwin as commanding general, in charge of running the entire training program of more than 60,000 soldiers. When Iraq invaded Kuwait in August 1990, the soldiers at the NTC were eager to deploy to the Gulf. They trained on tactics that simulated Iraqi trench warfare, and one group from the First Infantry Division finished the training program and was deployed by the time the United States began Operation Desert Storm in January 1991. In the remaining weeks of the war, the NTC prepared National Guard brigades for the fight.

Gen. John Yeosock of the USA Forces Command reported, "As the ARCENT [Army Central Command] commander, I see daily the results of [Clark's] efforts come to fruition here in Saudi Arabia.... He has the foresight to anticipate requirements and adapt to the changing world situation and has formulated initiatives to assure that the NTC continues to serve as the vital link in preparing the army to go to war. . . . Wes Clark's potential clearly exceeds that of his peers." Gen. Edwin Burba of the Headquarter Forces Command summed up Clark as the "best leader-thinker in the army."

Gen. Christman described Clark's work at the NTC as vital to the development of the new, post-Vietnam army. His improvements to the training itself, as well as the crucial new system for assessing senior officers, was put to the test on the battlefield and found very successful. "Wes was at the center of the entire training reform effort for the army," said Christman. "Everybody recognized that the performance of our young commanders in Desert Storm and Iraq were a direct reflection of training at the National Training Center, and Clark had been central to the success of the NTC."[37]

By the time Clark became commanding general at the NTC in 1989, his son was a college student at Georgetown University. Wesley Jr. would receive a bachelor's degree from the university's School of Foreign Service, then go on to spend four years in the army, including the Armor Officer Basic Course. While at Georgetown, he met a relative from his father's side of the family. April Kanne was also studying at the School of Foreign Service, and she and Wes Jr. introduced their parents to each other. In 1990, Clark met his cousin, Barry Kanne, for the first time. Kanne had founded a telecommunications business in Atlanta and, like Wes, was very interested in science and technology. Clark began to learn more about his Kanne ancestry through phone calls and visits to his cousin, and the families would continue to grow closer over the years.

Wes Jr. did not decide to follow in his father's footsteps, but worked in advertising in New York and eventually settled in Los Angeles to pursue a screenwriting career. He has written scripts on military themes, such as a cold war thriller and a story about air force para-rescue jumpers. As of the time of his father's Democratic nomination campaign, he had sold several projects to producers, but none had yet been produced by a movie studio.[38]

At the end of his command at Fort Irwin in 1991, Clark received another Legion of Merit award for his "personal efforts" that were "instrumental in maintaining the National Training Center as the United States Army's training centerpiece for both the present and future." He was promoted to major general, and his next duty was another tour on the army staff as deputy chief of staff for concepts, doctrine, and developments at Fort Monroe, Virginia. This base is headquarters for the army Training and Doctrine Command (TRADOC), and Clark's mission was, simply stated in his record, to "assist the commanding general in preparing the army for war and being the architect of the future." Here, he continued to help the modern, post–Cold War army evolve with new ideas in a wide range of areas, from organization to technology. "I told the chief of staff I needed an intellectual jump-start in combat developments and doctrine," wrote Gen. Frederick Franks. "Wes Clark provided that and then some."

Those developments included proposals for high-tech, digital electronic systems that would upgrade the speed and efficiency of combat maneuvers. The visual information collected by one soldier, for example, could be instantly relayed to every other level of command through a digital network. In an article for *Army* magazine, Clark called this new system "digitization of the battlefield." The army had been developing electronic communication systems and other technology for the past fifteen years, and Clark explained that the foundation for the next level had already been used in the large-scale data networks that connected troops and commanders in Desert Storm. He described his vision of more enhanced digitization as "streams of packetized information moving across national, theater and tactical grids as high-speed, computer-bit communications, rapid processing aided by expert systems and high-speed displays, and decision aids to solve the thorniest problems confronting landpower."[39]

With a broad knowledge of the military's capabilities and future direction, Clark set up discussions between the army and the air force about how they would cooperate on the battlefield. He was also selected to lead the army's delegation at British and French staff talks, an international duty he "served with great distinction."

Clark's performance at TRADOC earned him a top command post in the army as division commander of the First Cavalry Division at Fort Hood. In 1992, at age forty-three, the major general relocated to the historic post in central Texas, about 100 miles north of Austin. In Clark's mind, the First Cavalry had always stood out among the army's ten divisions. The division consisted of three brigades totaling 16,244 soldiers and over 6,000 tanks and other vehicles. Clark was responsible for making the division combat-ready, a job in the new army that, according to the military record, included "all aspects of training, maintaining, caring, and leading."

Commanding the First Cavalry was nothing like his previous "turnaround" assignments. Clark described the aura of excellence that surrounded Fort Hood:

> The "First Team," it was called: a full-strength division, recently returned from the Gulf War, placed at

the top of the army's priority list. It had a history, a great combat record, especially in Vietnam, and a tremendous esprit. This was an elite unit, with top-notch officers and sergeants at every level. It was a unit that just hummed with positive energy.[40]

The Horse Cavalry Detachment at Fort Hood is the last mounted cavalry unit in the army, and Clark got in the saddle to ride around the base from time to time. He made quality-of-life a priority in his officer training with the First Cavalry, and Army Corps Commanding Gen. Horace Taylor noted that "Clark has developed soldier-oriented leaders who are sensitive to both soldier and family needs." Clark applied the same command techniques he had used in the past, and saw the division win war games at the NTC and make its quotas for reenlistment. Combat-ready forces were crucial in this post–Desert Storm period, as the United States maintained a large force in the Gulf to contain Saddam Hussein from further aggression against Kuwait or his own people. Clark commanded three deployments from Fort Hood to Kuwait during his command. These "highly successful" deployments, according to Taylor, were "only possible due to [Clark's] establishment of a division-ready brigade structure that provided immediately deployable forces."

One of the off-the-base activities in which Clark participated during this period was the White House Fellows Commission, the board that selected upcoming fellows. In 1993 he was selected to the commission along with another Little Rock native, his childhood friend Mary Steenburgen. The actress was a friend of both Clark and Bill Clinton, and the commission brought the three of them together during a fellows-related trip in October 1993. "One of the things they have in common is me," said Steenburgen.[41]

In Clark's final Officer Evaluation Report for his command at Fort Hood, Gen. Dennis Reimer of the Army Headquarter Forces Command dubbed him "one of the army's best and brightest," and added that Clark "will continue to play a key role in leading the army into the 21st century." He was awarded the Distinguished Service Medal for "exceptionally meritorious service in a position of great responsibility," and the citation stated that Clark imbued the Division "with a singular spirit of duty, honor, and selfless service."

Clark left Fort Hood due to a promotion, but it had come as a surprise. By the spring of 1994, Clark had commanded the First Cavalry for two years and was looking forward to more. But the army had other ideas. During a base visit, Lt. Gen. Barry McCaffrey—a member of the Joint Staff in Washington and the most decorated general in the army—told Clark that he was leaving his post and recommending Clark for it.

Clark had previously heard some talk about a possible position for him in Washington. President Clinton had recently talked about him with the army chief of staff, referring to him as "my friend, Wes Clark." In his book *Waging Modern War*, Clark explained that, contrary to popular belief, he had merely been acquainted with the president by then.[42] They first met in 1965, when Clark was a senior at West Point and was visiting Georgetown University for a student conference. Clinton was class president at Georgetown, and Clark had been told that there was a fellow Arkansan at the school that he should meet. Clark was impressed; he had met hundreds of

Wesley Clark's father, Benjamin Jacob Kanne of Chicago. Kanne died just before Clark's fourth birthday.

Jacob and Ida Kanne, Clark's grandparents. The extended Kanne family gathered at their Chicago home every weekend.

*Wesley and his mother,
Veneta, in Chicago, 1945.*

*A toddler on the go in
Chicago, 1946.*

Four-year-old Wesley at a birthday party for his second-cousin, Mary Etzbach Campbell, who is in the center with her hand on her shoulder.

The former Clark home today in the Pulaski Heights neighborhood of Little Rock.

Wesley in his cowboy outfit.

Clark (front right), about ten years old, with his Baptist Training Union class at the Pulaski Heights Baptist Church.

One of the cabins at the Boys' Club camp outside Little Rock, where Clark worked as a counselor for several summers.

Receiving the Little Rock Boys' Club "Boy of the Year" award from the organization's board president, James Coates Jr. in February 1962.

Clark, third from the right in the first long row, at Boys' State in 1961. It was an honor to be selected to attend this week-long seminar on government, and Clark decided to apply to West Point after talking to a cadet who was serving as a counselor there.

Clark's senior photograph from the Hall High School yearbook.

The Hall High swimming team, which Clark founded and coached, practiced at the Boys' Club because the high school didn't have a pool. Pictured are (front, left to right) Charles Olmstead and Paul Fraziner; (back, left to right) Tom Hodges, Phillip McMath, and Wesley Clark.

Cadet Clark participating on a New York television Youth Forum.

Cadet Clark returned to Little Rock during his senior year to present Rodger T. Rogers with the Fred W. Allsopp Newsboy of the Year Award. Clark had also been a recipient of the award, which was based on "performance as a newspaperboy, school achievement and good citizenship." Days earlier, Clark learned that he had won a Rhodes scholarship to attend Oxford after graduating from West Point. The star on Clark's collar signifies that he is a Distinguished Cadet, ranking in the top 5 percent of his class.

Victor Clark, right, accepts an award for his son at the West Point class of 1966 pre-graduation awards ceremony. Wesley could not attend because he was in the hospital with corneal abrasions caused by wearing his contacts too long. General Julio Pacheco, left, presented Victor Clark with the Peruvian Army Award, given to the cadet standing first in General Order of Merit—the top of the class.

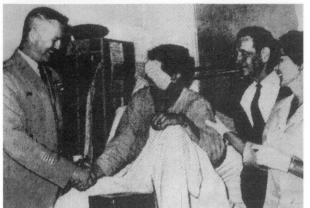

Eye-bandaged Clark in the hospital on award day, visited by West Point Superintendent Maj. Gen. Donald V. Bennett, left; and his parents, Victor and Veneta Clark.

Graduation day at West Point. Clark finished first in the class of 1966.

Clark's girlfriend Gert Kingston and his mother at his West Point graduation, June 1966. Gert, a native of Brooklyn, met Clark at a party in New York City while he was a cadet.

Clark at Oxford in April 1967 with his Morgan coupe.

Mr. and Mrs. Wesley Clark in the living room at Clark's childhood home in Little Rock in October 1968. Clark had just finished his Armor Officer Basic Course and was on his way to Ranger School.

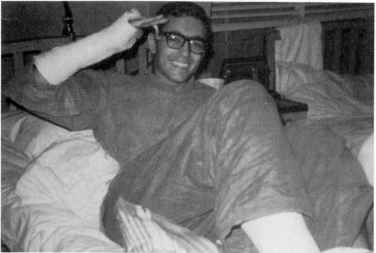

Recovering after surgery in the hospital at Camp Zama, Japan, in March 1970. Clark was awarded the Silver Star for gallantry after being shot in Vietnam.

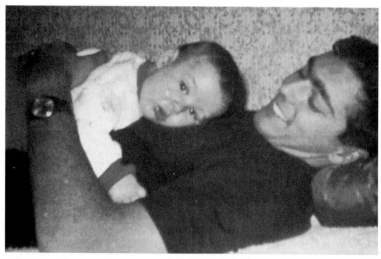

With Wesley Jr. at Fort Knox, Kentucky, in August 1970. Clark's son was born while he was in Vietnam.

The family at Fort Carson, Colorado, in June 1982, where Lieutenant Colonel Clark was Commander of the First Battalion, Seventy-Seventh Armor, Fourth Infantry Division.

Lieutenant Colonel Clark takes the baton in a two-mile relay in a competition at the U.S. Army War College at Carlisle Barracks, Pennsylvania, April 1983.

Mom and Dad proudly pin the gold bars on the shoulders of Second Lt. Wesley Clark Jr. at Georgetown University in May 1992.

Chateau Gendebien in Mons, Belgium, General Clark's headquarters as Supreme Allied Commander Europe (SACEUR).

General Clark, President Bill Clinton, and NATO Sec. Gen. Javier Solana during the president's trip to NATO headquarters on May 5, 1999.

NATO Secretary General Javier Solana embraces Gen. Wesley Clark (right), U.S. Army, SACEUR, after an award ceremony for Solana in the Pentagon on Sept. 23, 1999.

SACEUR Gen. Wesley Clark talks to First Lt. Jeffrey Csoka during Thanksgiving dinner at the Comanche Inn on Comanche Base, Tuzla, Bosnia and Herzegovina, on Nov. 25, 1999. Clark visited the troops in the field during the holiday.

The SACEUR briefs reporters on the status of the NATO-led, international peacekeeping operation in Bosnia and Herzegovina at the Pentagon on Dec. 9, 1999.

General Clark with a crowd of Albanians after Serb forces were driven out of Kosovo.

Wavecrest

Clark (center) talks about the development of the Wavecrest electric bike with Mike Fritz (left), vice president of product development, and Chris Washburn, vice president and general manager, light transport, at Wavecrest's headquarters in Dulles, Virginia.

Antonia Felix

Gert Clark at a campaign fundraiser in New York City, December 2003.

Antonia Felix

With Rep. Charles Rangel at his left and a group of local leaders on the podium behind, Clark greets the audience at a rally in Harlem on December 11, 2003.

AP/Wide World/EPA/Andrew Gombert

On February 13, 2004, Clark gives United States Senator and Democratic Presidential hopeful John Kerry, left, his endorsement at a University of Wisconsin rally in Madison.

smart college men at debate meets, but Clinton struck him as "the most impressive man I'd met on the college circuit in three years of traveling around." When Clark told this story during his Democratic nomination campaign in 2003, he liked to remark that Clinton came into the room that first day with a girl on each arm.[43] Clark had dinner with the Clintons in Little Rock when Clinton was governor, and had spoken to him on the phone a few later, but "that was about the extent of it."[44]

The job that McCaffrey was leaving was the J5, a senior position on the Joint Staff that deals with political-military affairs around the world. This job would take Clark beyond the army to the full spectrum of U.S. military strategic plans, and it was a three-star position. Clark was called to Washington for an interview with the new chairman of the Joint Chiefs, John Shalikashvili ("Shali"). He thought that it went well, but before leaving the Joint Chief's office he learned that he was not the army nominee for the job. With ten other senior officers, he was simply listed as available for the post. He felt "slightly adrift, like when you were expecting an A on your report card but got a B−," he recalled. Clark's career history and McCaffrey's endorsement had worked in his favor, however; a few weeks later Shalikashvili called and asked him when he could start.

Clark was promoted to lieutenant general when he was named J5, and in the spring of 1994 he and Gert left Texas for Washington, DC. Christman, who had worked with Clark on the faculty at West Point, would work with him again in this post. Christman served as assistant to the chairman, and he explained that working for the Joint Chiefs had become much more significant by that time in terms of one's career track due to new legislation that was enacted in 1986. By issuing the Goldwater-Nichols Department of Defense Reorganization Act, the congressional defense advocates for reform "said that it was time to change the ethic, to make jointness truly a litmus test for officer success," said Christman. "As a result, when Clark and I joined the staff, it was perceived throughout the military as an extremely prestigious spot. The two most important positions were the J3, operations, and the J5. Clark's position was looked upon as extremely important for a three-star officer."[45]

Clark's first days were a hands-on immersion course in U.S. foreign policy, as he delved into crises that flared up all over the globe. Immediate concerns were North Korea's nuclear capability, relief for Kurds in Northern Iraq, genocide in Rwanda, a potential U.S. embargo of Haiti, and plans for the remaining U.S. troops in Somalia. In addition, Clark was responsible for creating a document for Congress that defined the country's military strategy. And underlying everything was the fighting in Bosnia, where the power struggle between the multiethnic republics of the former Yugoslavia continued to erupt in chaos and bloodshed. "The weekend I got there our aircraft were dropping bombs in Bosnia as part of a NATO mission to attack the Serbs that were shelling Gorazde. I've never seen anything like it," Clark said.[46]

In 1992, the year before Clinton took office, Bosnia was the scene of a brutal war in which Serbian forces committed ethnic cleansing, killing tens of thousands and driving more than a million Muslims and Croats from their homes. As the world learned about the Serbian concentration camps, where rape and other atrocities were committed, and about the tragic conditions of the millions of refugees forced to leave their villages, the pressure was on to bring peace to the area before it threatened the security of Europe. Slobodan Milosevic, president of neighboring Serbia, had begun to inflame nationalistic Serbian ideas years earlier in his role as a communist leader in Yugoslavia, and these hostilities drove a path to war in the region. The Clinton administration struggled with a policy toward Bosnia.

When Clark arrived at the Pentagon in 1994, he began working on a policy paper to outline the military options to help resolve the conflict. That summer, he traveled to Bosnia to meet the military leaders on both sides of the war in order to collect information for "a proper policy analysis." He met with Maj. Gen. Rasim Delic, the Bosnian Muslim commander, as well as Gen. Ratko Mladic, the Bosnian Serb commander. Mladic would later be indicted for war crimes against the Muslims and Croats, and Clark quickly suffered fallout for the meeting. The *Washington Post* reported that Clark visited Mladic in spite of a "warning" issued by the U.S. ambassador to Bosnia. The paper also carried a photograph of Clark exchanging hats with the Serb general, which also spurred controversy.[47]

Clark had listed the visit in the itinerary he submitted to Ambassador Chuck Redmond, but later learned that he hadn't approved the visit. Clark explained that the *Washington Post* article was wrong—there had not been a warning and he had not been instructed to cancel the meeting—but the damage had been done. Two congressmen called for his dismissal, but Clark was supported by those in the Defense Department and the National Security Council staff who understood his motivations for meeting the general. Clark explained, "How many people, I reflected at the time, have the opportunity to size up a potential adversary face-to-face?" President Clinton defended Clark with a letter to Congress, and the contro-

versy ended shortly afterward. "It was my first experience in the rough and tumble of high visibility," said
Clark, "and a painful few days."[48]

In 1995, Secretary of Defense William Perry set up an
American negotiating team to work on a peace agreement
between the warring factions in Bosnia. He chose
Richard Holbrooke, assistant secretary of state for
European and Canadian affairs, to lead the group.
Formerly the U.S. ambassador to Germany, Holbrooke
had a background in government and diplomacy extending back to six years of staff posts in Vietnam. Clark
joined the team as the military adviser, and they set out
to Europe in August to meet with American allies about
the plan and begin talks with Bosnian leaders. Clark's
role was to represent General Shalikashvili, and it was a
significant new turn in his career. "This was my first time
to be the front man in selling a plan," he wrote, "dealing
with international military and diplomatic counter-
parts."[49] The biggest selling point for their plan was the
promise of 25,000 U.S. troops to help keep the peace.
Clark's job was to analyze exactly how those troops would
be used.

In *To End a War*, Holbrooke described Clark's unique
position as part of the negotiating team:

> "He was in a complicated position on our team. . . .
> With three stars, Clark was at the crossroads of his
> career; this assignment would lead him either to a
> fourth star—every general officer's dream—or to
> retirement. Assignment to a diplomatic negotiating
> team offered some exciting possibilities, but it
> could be hazardous duty for a military officer, since
> it might put him into career-endangering conflicts
> with more senior officers. Clark's boyish demeanor
> and charm masked, but only slightly, his extraordi-

nary intensity. No one worked longer hours or pushed himself harder than Wes Clark. Great things were expected of him—and he expected them of himself."[50]

The team's trip started tragically. At the end of the first week, the group had an accident while driving on a dangerous road heading toward Sarajevo, the Bosnian capital. The red-dirt road that crossed over Mount Igman was one of the worst in Europe; rough, narrow, and unstable due to little or no foundation. Its unprotected sides led to drop-offs down the mountain, and certain areas of the road were patrolled by Serbian soldiers who were known to shoot at U.N. vehicles. Milosevic had refused to call off his gunners or to guarantee their security on the road, so no one was looking forward to the drive.

The group was traveling in two vehicles—a large, heavily armored personnel carrier, painted white to signify the United Nations, and an army Humvee. Clark rode in the Humvee with Holbrooke, Lt. Col. Randy Banky, and the driver. Another group, including three senior members of the negotiating team, rode in the big personnel carrier. These three were Robert C. Frasure, Holbrooke's deputy and former American ambassador to Estonia; Joseph J. Kruzel, deputy assistant secretary of defense; and Air Force Col. Samuel Nelson Drew. Earlier in the week, as everyone got to know each other, Clark and Kruzel had taken a dare of the group and dived out of their third-story hotel window into the Adriatic Sea.

On a steep and narrow section of the mountain road, an edge of the crumbling road gave way beneath the white personnel carrier. It fell off the cliff and somersaulted down the side of the mountain. Clark and Holbrooke were ahead, passing a convoy of French tanks going the other direction. One of the drivers stopped to tell them that a vehicle behind them had gone off the road. Clark and Holbrooke ran back to the spot where the roadside had fallen apart. They began to crawl down the mountain, but were driven back up by gunfire from unseen snipers, as well as from shouts from the French soldiers warning them that the area was full of mines. The personnel carrier had fallen down to the road below, beyond the last hairpin turn they had taken. The gunfire stopped, and Clark and Holbrooke ran around the curve and farther down the road. They realized that the vehicle had bounced off the road and dropped down the next section of mountain. French vehicles, including a medical unit, were gathered at the spot. Clark and Holbrooke tied a rope around a tree, and Clark rappelled down the mountain to get to the vehicle.

The vehicle was on fire when he reached it, apparently from exploding ammunition that it had been carrying. Two wounded Americans had been dragged away by Bosnian soldiers and taken to a hospital before he arrived, and Clark saw the charred remains of two others, later identified as Robert C. Frasure and Sam Nelson Drew. Holbrooke and others feared for Clark's safety because of the fire and the landmines. They shouted down to him, pleading with him to crawl back up to the road, but the combat soldier in Clark refused to leave the bodies. "I stayed to make sure the remains were properly removed," he said.[51] They soon learned that one of the hospitalized Americans, Joe Kruzel, also died. Holbrooke recalled that Clark looked ten years older when he climbed back up. "It's the worst thing you've ever seen down there," Clark told him.[52]

The team returned to Washington for the memorial ceremony for Frasure, Kruzel, and Drew, but afterward the negotiations forged ahead. Holbrooke's plan was ultimately agreed upon by the Bosnians and Serbs at talks in the United States in late 1995. The agreement divided Bosnia into two semi-autonomous sections, 51 percent to a new Croat-Muslim Federation and 49 percent to a Serbian leadership. A NATO peacekeeping force of 60,000 troops and personnel, including 20,000 Americans, was also accepted by all parties. The peace agreement, which was developed at the Wright-Patterson Air Force Base in Dayton, Ohio, was signed on December 14, 1995. The Dayton Peace Agreement stopped the fighting in Bosnia, but it did not solve the problems in the Balkans definitively, as Clark would learn in a future command.

During the negotiations, Clark spent many hours with Milosevic and came to sum him up as "a supremely manipulative liar and bully."[53] At one dinner, Milosevic turned to Clark and asked how soon the NATO troops would arrive after the agreement was put into effect. "It would be better if it were not soon," he told Clark. "Serb people are proud, and it will take time to accustom them to outside force."

"Mr. President," answered Clark, "The forces will come almost immediately after the agreement goes into effect. They will be here very soon."

"Then it would be best if they would come in small numbers," he replied.

"Well, they will come in large numbers, Mr. President, and they will come soon," said Clark. "It is the way it has to be done. That way there will be no doubt about their capabilities. And the agreement will thus be respected." After that exchange, Milosevic grunted and returned to his dinner.[54]

"When the chips were down in Bosnia ... in the summer of 1995, nations turned to NATO," Clark said in 2000. "NATO and American leadership ... [put] pressure on the Serbs through the use of airpower that brought about the Dayton peace process. NATO and American leadership and 20,000 U.S. soldiers who crossed the Sava River in winter provided the fundamental foundation that helped stop the fighting in a war-torn land."[55] Among Clark's contributions at Dayton was finding a safe land route between Sarajevo and Gorazde that would be acceptable to the Serbs. This route came to be known to the U.S. team as the "Clark Corridor," and Holbrooke described it as an important break in the Dayton negotiations.[56]

Clark's two-year assignment as J5 prepared him for an upcoming command that would again place him in the middle of a crisis in the Balkans. But the three-star post had a two-year time limit, and the end of that period was coming up in April 1996. If he did not receive another assignment, his only choice would be to retire. But at fifty-one, he was in perfect shape and ready for another command. He received one, but like the situation surrounding his J5 appointment, he was not the first man considered for the job.

✯ ✯ ✯ ✯

SIX

Four Stars

"In the fall of 1962 as a plebe, he had begun his career in the army as a wunderkind and had ended it, thirty-seven years later, as a four-star and the American commander of NATO forces in Kosovo, still in a way a wunderkind, as bright and brash as the first day he arrived at West Point, ready to take on the world."

—David Halberstam,
War in a Time of Peace[1]

In his second year as J5 at the Pentagon, Clark began thinking about what he would do after retiring from the army. "Under the army system, promotion to three stars starts the clock ticking," he said. At the end of two years in that position, he would either be asked to serve another year as J5, get promoted to another post, or leave Washington with a copy of his retirement papers. At the beginning of 1996, Clark wasn't optimistic about his chances for promotion because he heard that the army chief of staff, Gen. Dennis Reimer, did not want to promote him to a full four-star general. "As might be expected," Clark noted, "no specific reason was given."[2]

The "marked man" quality that Clark sensed as early as West Point continued to haunt him, even after rounding out thirty exceptional years of service in the army with his important contribution to the Dayton Peace Agreement. He had made new political alliances as J5 in Richard Holbrooke, Madeleine Albright, and Clinton's National Security Adviser Sandy Berger. He was among a committed group of innovators who had dedicated themselves to building the modern army. But Reimer's spurn drove home another reality of the new army—officers like Clark who were advanced quickly and excelled in the academic as well as military phases of training—were looked upon suspiciously as "water-walkers." Gen. Robert Scales admits that Clark, with such a well-known reputation as one of the army's brightest, may be the object of resentment among some. "I can't think of anyone in my thirty-four years in the army who is even remotely close to Wes in raw intellectual power," he said. "If anyone comes close it would be Colin Powell; he's a brilliant man. But in terms of the ability to assimilate facts and play those facts back in some way to see things in new and imaginative ways, Wes is in a different league. Nobody comes close to him in that regard, and frankly it creates resentment."[3]

Scales described Clark as someone who does not cover up his intellectual nature beneath a backslapping persona. "Wes is not the sort of guy who shirks intellectual challenges," he said. "He is a very straightforward guy. But then again nobody works harder than Wes does, either. Maybe part of it is that he's not adhering enough to the culture. There is an aspect of the army, a country boy, tobacco-chewing aspect that holds that if you're a real combat leader you're supposed to have this good-old-boy personality. Clark uses words with more than three syllables, and he doesn't come off that way."[4]

John "Jack" Wheeler, one of Clark's West Point classmates and longtime friends, offered a poignant view of

Clark's conflicts with army culture. "Clark's wonderful gifts," he said, "his extremely rapid ability to assimilate information and conclude consequences, are blessings. This comes from the French, *blessure*, or wound, which is one way to say that his gift was powerfully two-sided. Inevitably there would be envy. He's got a Pentium chip to operate with, ready to act in nanoseconds, while everybody else is using their little Apple II, and it takes us a while to figure something out. Wes sits there knowing where we're going. He has to live with that. And he does it admirably."[5]

Allen Andersson, a Washington-based entrepreneur who worked with Clark in the early 2000s, also describes him as a well-spoken intellectual. "He's very straightforward and speaks in sophisticated language, but expresses things simply," he said. "Although he's a man of action and a very practical person—you can't win a war without being active and practical—he is most of all an intellectual, a person who thinks independently, clearly; who finds the greatest kind of pleasure in making his mind work. He works with ideas, he's open minded; he's willing to think opposite thoughts within ten seconds of one another to see how they work with one another. I think that if he asked himself to name his proudest accomplishment in the army, he may say it was as a junior colonel and general, being one of the military intellectuals who did advanced thinking about what the army should look like, what a battlefield should look like in twenty years and what they should do to prepare it. When we saw the U.S. Army go into action on the ground for the first time in a long time in late 2001, the startling effectiveness of small teams on the ground backed up by sophisticated systems was largely a product of the processes that Wes put in place. Success has a million fathers, and Wes Clark rightly claims much of that father-hood."[6]

Holbrooke summed up the animosity that developed between Clark and some senior military officials this way: "It is extremely simple: jealous generals. And it goes back to way before Kosovo. . . . Wes Clark is a water-walker, Rhodes scholar, top-of-his-class 'brown-noser' in the eyes of the tougher, more manly men in uniform."[7]

In spite of the rumor that General Reimer did not want Clark promoted, in March 1996 Clark was named to the four-star post of commander in chief of the U.S. Southern Command (SOUTHCOM), based in Panama. He was not the army's original nominee for the position, but the other officer "hadn't been accepted for some reason," explained Clark, and subsequently General Shalikashvili signed Clark's promotion order and Congress approved his nomination.[8] SOUTHCOM is one of the army's five geographical regions of operation, and its area of responsibility includes the thirty-two nations in Central and South America and the Caribbean. Personnel-wise, SOUTHCOM is a small command with about 3,000 permanent military and civilian people assigned. "It was an ideal charge with which to learn the duties of a regional commander in chief [CINC]," said Clark.[9]

Clark took on an intense study of Spanish when he learned he would be taking over this command. When he gained some facility in it, he became multilingual in three foreign languages. Seven years later, when making a television commercial for his Democratic nomination campaign, he fretted over what to say about his foreign language abilities. "I debated this really hard about these four languages [English being the fourth]," he said. "I know a little bit of Russian, a little bit of German, and a [*poquito*] *español*. Where I am right now is I can still read a Spanish newspaper, and I can give a speech in German if it's written out. And with two vodkas, I can still talk sports in Russian."[10]

Clark visited most of the countries covered by SOUTHCOM, and also traveled to Washington, DC, regularly to report to Secretary of Defense William Perry. He met military leaders in Colombia and witnessed the corruption throughout the leadership of the country. "They've never had a chance to live under the kind of equal-opportunity government that we pride ourselves on here in America," he said in a speech in 2003. "I think the ultimate answer in South America is to bring prosperity, bring American know-how down there." He applauded President Bush's call for a North American Free Trade Agreement, and added, "I don't think there's a military solution to it."[11]

Army headquarters and troops were scheduled to leave the Panama Canal Zone on December 31, 1999, when control of the area would return to Panama. Clark argued for the relocation of the U.S. troops to Puerto Rico rather than to Fort Gillem, Georgia, which Reimer proposed as the most inexpensive solution as there were unused facilities there. Clark thought it was important to keep the command in a Spanish-speaking region and in closer proximity to Latin America and the rest of the nations in SOUTHCOM territory. Eventually, Shalikashvili agreed with Clark's plan to move the command to Fort Buchanan, Puerto Rico.

Less than a year into his assignment in Panama, Clark was brought to Washington to interview with Secretary of Defense William Cohen about another command that was coming available in the summer of 1997. Gen. George Joulwan was to retire as Commander in Chief,

U.S. European Command (CINCEUR), the top command in the U.S. military. This is the double-bill command in which the commander also serves NATO as Supreme Allied Commander Europe (SACEUR). Clark had worked at the command headquarters when he served under CINCEUR/SACEUR Alexander Haig about twenty years earlier.

Again, Clark was on a list of officers available for the post, but was not the army's nominee. The army had tapped Lt. Gen. Marc Cisneros for the job; seven years earlier, he had led the United States' successful invasion of Panama. According to Cisneros, Clark's close relationships with Shalikashvili and Clinton won him the post, and he remains bitter about Clark's promotion. "I personally think Clark was told he was not going to get promoted, but he was buddies with Clinton," said Cisneros.[12] At the time Clark and Cisneros discussed the SACEUR position, Clark told Cisneros that the job was his for the taking; according to Clark, this was the information he had at the time of their conversation. Shalikashvili remarked that he had intervened on Clark's behalf for the SACEUR post, just as he had done to get him the command in Panama. "Again, as it was with SOUTHCOM, there were a number of people nominated by the other branches," Shalikashvili said, "and the army had also another individual. I had a very strong role in [Clark's] last two jobs."[13] The contention that arose between Clark and Cisneros—which also led to animosity toward Clark from other senior officers—focused upon whether or not Clark knew that Shalikashvili was working to get him the post at the time he spoke to Cisneros about it. Clark denies that he did, yet Cisneros' unhappiness over the incident was well-known.

Clark won congressional and North Atlantic Council

approval for the post, and on July 10, 1997, he and Gert moved to the command's opulent headquarters at Chateau Gendebien in Mons, Belgium, a 23-acre estate complete with tennis courts, greenhouses, and gardeners. In his press release about Clark's appointment, President Clinton said that Clark had had "a long and distinguished career spanning three decades, with significant policy and diplomatic experience as well as impeccable credentials as a military commander.... I look forward to General Clark continuing the work of General Joulwan as [the] SACEUR takes on the challenge of guiding NATO military forces through this important period of transition and the completion of NATO's stabilization force in Bosnia."[14]

At the change-of-command flag ceremony, Clark became responsible for 109,000 American troops, their 150,000 family members, and 50,000 civilians who comprised the American military in Europe, most of Africa, and part of the Middle East, including Israel. If the need arose, he also had a seven-million-strong NATO force at his command. "There was a brief instant, as I took the flag from Shali, when I felt the weight of command responsibility descend," said Clark.[15]

As SACEUR, Clark had a personal staff of about 100 at Supreme Headquarters Allied Powers Europe (SHAPE), including eleven special assistants, twelve security agents, five drivers, and four schedulers. A separate staff handled the day-to-day maintenance of the chateau. For transportation, he had his own DC-9, two Blackhawk helicopters and two armored Mercedes.

Clark, who reported to NATO Secretary General Javier Solana and to President Clinton, was responsible for balancing the strategy of the nineteen NATO nations with that of Washington. His channel to Clinton went through both Secretary of Defense William Cohen and the new chairman of the Joint Chiefs of Staff, Gen. Hugh Shelton (his ally, Shalikashvili, had retired). He would also work closely with the vice chairman of the Joint Chiefs, Gen. Joseph Ralston. From the start, the challenges of this already complex command were further deepened by the rift between the Pentagon and the White House over a strategy in the Balkans. Shelton, Cohen, and other military leaders wanted to limit U.S. involvement, in fear of another muddy and horrible engagement like Vietnam. Many in the Clinton administration, however, including Secretary of State Madeleine Albright, wanted to strike hard at Milosevic to put a halt to the brutality and ethnic cleansing that the Dayton Peace Agreement had failed to do in 1995. Albright was hawkish on potential U.S. involvement in Kosovo, and Clark agreed with her. Their alliance had been building for years; Clark was Albright's military adviser when she was the U.S. ambassador to the United Nations, and Clark's son had taken classes from Albright at Georgetown University.

Clinton's foreign policy stance leaned toward intervention for humanitarian and ethical reasons, a position that clashed with the military's post-Vietnam reluctance to engage. Therefore, he had a difficult time forming a strategy for Kosovo. In October 1998, the United Nations issued Resolution 1199 demanding that the hostilities cease in Kosovo, and Holbrooke began trying to negotiate a peace. He was not successful, but a massacre in the Balkans in January 1999 brought the brutality of Serbian aggression to the world stage once again and forced the issue. Nations were shocked by the brutal tactics of the Serbs against the Albanians in the village of Racak, where forty-five Albanians were rounded up and executed.

(The Albanians formed the biggest population of the Serbian principality of Kosovo, but were led by a Serbian minority. Among their cultural and religious differences, the Serbs are Orthodox Christians, while most of the Albanians are Muslims.) NATO was forced to act, and Clark's 100-plus hours of previous contact with Serbian leader Milosevic assured him that a strong show of force—a bombing campaign—would halt his aggression as it had done previously in Bosnia. Clinton described the mission in humanitarian terms: "This is not a defeat for Serbia we're seeking. What we're seeking is the simple fight of the Kosovar Albanians to live in peace on their own land, without fear of cleansing because of their religious or their ethnic background, and a simple statement that in Europe there will be no more ethnic cleansings. We will not usher in the 21st century with the worst nightmare of the 20th."[16]

Clark's pro-interventionist attitude had been stoked by the United States' refusal to intervene in Rwanda in 1994, when escalating tribal warfare resulted in the Hutus murdering approximately 800,000 Tutsis. He felt it would be another immoral act to ignore the ethnic cleansing in Kosovo, and this attitude made him the perfect military leader to ally with Clinton and Albright. Holbrooke, who had again been chosen as the U.S. special envoy to the Balkans, considered Clark the perfect choice for SACEUR because "he was essentially a liberal interventionist, forward-leaning in the use of national power."[17] Clark was committed to showing Milosevic a strong hand, and pledged to "systematically and progressively attack, disrupt, degrade, devastate, [and] ultimately destroy" the Serbian military if Milosevic did not halt his attacks.[18]

After the Serbian attack at Racak, Albright tried to

build a diplomatic solution between the Serbs and Albanians at a conference at Rambouillet, a chateau near Paris. When that failed, Holbrooke met with Milosevic in Belgrade to offer him one last opportunity to step back, but the leader refused. "You understand what will happen when I leave," Holbrooke told him. "Yes," Milosevic said, "You'll bomb us. You're a big, powerful country and you can do anything you want, and there is nothing we can do about it." Holbrooke told him that the action "will be swift, it will be severe, and it will be sustained."[19]

Clark, who joined Holbrooke in the talks, recalled pulling Milosevic aside one evening and saying, "Mr. President, you have to understand that NATO is very serious. You have to pull out the excess forces. If you don't there's an activation order. And if they tell me to bomb you, I'm going to bomb you good." Clark then described Milosevic's chilling justification for his actions against the Albanians, whom he called "murderers and bandits." The Serbian leader said that he knew how to handle them. Decades earlier, his solution had been "killing them all, although it took several years, we killed them all."[20]

As the military head of NATO, Clark ordered the bombing to begin on March 24, 1999, to enforce U.N. Resolution 1199. By that time, Serbs had forced approximately 100,000 from their homes in Kosovo, and Albright summed up Milosevic's goals as fourfold: to "exterminate the KLA [the Albanian counterattack force], reengineer Kosovo's ethnic balance on a permanent basis, frighten into submission the Albanians who remained in Kosovo, and create a destabilizing humanitarian crisis that would preoccupy the international community and divide the region."[21]

Clark and other strategists assumed that Milosevic

would give quickly, but the Serbian defense put up a stronger fight than anyone had anticipated. United States leaders and NATO would only commit to an air campaign; no one wanted to bring in ground forces and increase the odds of allied casualties. Clark felt that this contributed to Milosevic's refusal to stand down, and his repeated requests for a more stepped up effort—such as to bring in Blackhawk helicopters—further strained his relationship with the Pentagon.

Secretary Cohen was not pleased with Clark's strong alliances at the White House and felt that he was circumventing the Pentagon to push through his own strategy. Clark's supposed close ties to Clinton fed this resentment, even though their relationship was exaggerated. There were several parallels in their nearly simultaneous careers: Both were Arkansans raised by stepfathers and strong, supportive mothers who nurtured their ambitions; both had brilliant intellects and were Rhodes scholars; and both rose quickly in their careers. Although many assumed, based on these similarities, that they were long-time friends, in reality their paths had not intersected very often. The military, which has traditionally been conservative, was critical of Clinton for his lack of military experience and his promotion of a policy to allow gays in the military. In their eyes, Clark's alleged alliance with Clinton was a red flag indicating that his loyalties may belong more to the White House than to the Pentagon.

The bombing campaign wore on week after week, with target sites that Clark felt were insufficient to move Milosevic. As Halberstam writes, it was a high-tech, surreal type of warfare, with invisible B-2 Stealth bombers flying at 15,000 feet and launching laser-guided weapons. "The war, amazingly futuristic in the eyes of men who

had fought in other wars, was obviously worthy of a science fiction novel. . . . The new technology of airpower
was performing brilliantly—well above expectations—
but because the target lists were so limited, the war was
going poorly."²² Clark grew frustrated with the lines of
communication between him and the National
Command Authority—the combination of the president
and the secretary of defense. He did not think he was
being brought into strategy discussions enough:
"Somehow, I had become just a NATO officer who also
reported to the United States," he wrote in *Waging
Modern War.* "I provided information and took orders, but
without engaging in give-and-take political-military discussions, we didn't seem to be making full use of the
unique potential of the SACEUR position."²³ These
problems became public as the media covered the war. In
an article entitled "War's Conduct Creates Tension
Among Chiefs," the *New York Times* reported that "ten-
sions have emerged. General Clark's aides say that the
Pentagon's caution and checks and balances clash with
his war-fighter's urgency to press the fight."²⁴

In the second month of the bombing campaign,
NATO members met for a summit in Washington to com-
memorate the fiftieth anniversary of the organization.
Clark's deteriorating relationship with the Pentagon was
evident in that he was not invited to attend—a scan-
dalous omission in light of the SACEUR's role. Clark's
repeated calls to formulate a ground campaign did not
bode well with the military, but he was adamant that
NATO needed to up the ante in order for the Serbs to
retreat before winter. The Serbs had driven 900,000
refugees from their homes by this point, many of whom
were struggling to survive out in the open. If Milosevic
didn't clear his troops out soon, the forecast for their sur-

vival was bleak. Clark enlisted Secretary General Solana's help in getting him to the summit, and he was finally approved to attend. When he arrived, Secretary Cohen specifically ordered him to refrain from talking about the ground troops issue. "Nothing about ground forces. We have to make this air campaign work, or we'll both be writing our resumes," he told Clark. "Yes, sir," Clark responded. "I'm not going to spoil the summit. I'm not going to be the skunk at the picnic."[25]

At the summit, the Clinton administration resolved to step up their efforts and allowed the target list to be expanded. Clark returned to Belgium and kept the press apprised of the operation in a series of press conferences. At one such briefing, his comment about the number of Serbian troops elicited headlines such as "NATO Chief Admits Bombs Fail to Stem Serb Operations," which prompted severe fallout from the Pentagon. Clark called the reporters' spin "a complete misunderstanding of my statement and of the facts," but he got a call from General Shelton the next night. Clark related the call in his book:

> "Wes, at the White House meeting today there was a lot of discussion about your press conference," Shelton began. "The Secretary of Defense asked me to give you some verbatim guidance, so here it is: 'Get your f——ing face off the TV. No more briefings, period. That's it.' I just wanted to give it to you like he said it. Do you have any questions?"[26]

Clark remarked that Clinton read the transcript of the press release as well as the newspaper articles that followed, and agreed with Clark that his statements had been misconstrued. But this episode is one example of the difficult relationship Clark had with the military leadership back home.

Clark continued to work on a ground troops plan in order to have something in place if bombing strikes alone failed to make Milosevic surrender. The White House began to seriously consider such a plan as part of its stepped-up commitment to the war. In early May, the administration's new determination was put into action with an order to increase the number of bombing targets, and from that point Milosevic realized that NATO's resolve was not weakening, as he had assumed it would, but rather strengthening. In addition, the military and diplomatic aid he had expected from Russia was not coming. In spite of Russia's previous alliances with the Serbs, it was too dependent upon the West to create a divide over them. This stark reality was compounded by other factors working against Milosevic, including an increase in desertions from his own Serb army, the threat of NATO ground troops coming into Kosovo, and the devastating effects of the bombing on his military, economic, and political structures.

On May 27, a U.N. tribunal indicted Milosevic as a war criminal. At the same time, the G-7 countries were working on a proposal that called for all Serb soldiers, police, and paramilitary personnel to leave Kosovo and be replaced by peacekeeping forces. The Russian envoys at the negotiations stalled for a while, hoping to allow some Serb troops to remain, but on orders of the Kremlin they ultimately agreed to the "all Serb forces out" provision and signed the agreement. When Viktor Chernomyrdin, a former Russian prime minister, and Martti Ahtisaari, the president of Finland, met with Milosevic to discuss the agreement, they made it clear that "the Russians were now, in effect, on the other side, and the game was over. . . . It was the best deal he could get . . . he had better take it because anything else was going to be worse."[27]

The next day, June 4, Milosevic signed the agreement. His surrender proved that the high-tech air war capabilities that had developed since the Gulf War had changed military history. Halberstam quotes military historian John Keegan on this point: "There are certain dates in the history of warfare that mark real turning points.... A new turning point to fix on the calendar [is] June 3, 1999, when the capitulation of President Milosevic proved that a war can be won by airpower alone."[28]

On June 10, the Serbian forces began to withdraw and NATO continued to work on plans for letting their peacekeeping troops in. Clark later stated that this date was a deadline he had devised in order to fulfill orders from Washington to end the war that summer, before Vice President Al Gore began his presidential campaign. In a January 2000 interview with a NATO historian, Clark described the political aspect that played out at the end of the conflict. "There were those in the White House who said, 'Hey, look, you gotta finish the bombing before the Fourth of July weekend. That's the start of the next presidential campaign season, so stop it.'" When Clark released these records in 2004 he did not name the officials involved, and Sandy Berger, who had been Clinton's national security adviser, said that although Clark was a friend his implications about such a political maneuver were "categorically and completely false." Gore did, however, launch his campaign one week after the war ended, on June 16, 1999.[29]

The Russians had hoped to police their own section of Kosovo, independent of NATO, as part of the settlement. When this did not get written into the plan, they began moving 200 troops toward the Pristina airport and Clark called NATO Secretary General Solana to discuss the issue. If the Russians got to the airport first, it could ignite a power struggle between Russia and NATO that would derail the entire peacekeeping process. Clark received permission from Solana to call 500 British and French paratroopers to occupy the airport and prevent the Russians from entering. But British General Sir Mike Jackson, the British peacekeeping force commander, would not allow it. "I'm not going to start the Third World War for you," he reportedly told Clark.[30]

When the Russians moved in and took over the airport, Clark asked Jackson for tanks and armored cars to block the runways so that the Russian planes that were scheduled to arrive could not land. Jackson refused him again, and Clark went to the leaders of Hungary, Romania, and Bulgaria to establish a no-fly zone to prevent the Russians from flying to Pristina. The order went through, and Russia's two transport planes, which carried 120 paratroopers, were not able to fly their mission. NATO then held talks with Russia to clarify what kind of patrols they could have in northern Kosovo. "The airlift's delay delivered NATO's latest blow to Russia's touchy pride and caused consternation in Moscow official circles, where many believe Russian presence in Kosovo serves as a security guarantee for Russia's Serb allies," reported the *Moscow Times* in July 1999.[31]

Although Clark's request for action at the airport was authorized and viable, Jackson's comment to him about World War III came back to haunt him a few years later. During Clark's campaign for the Democratic nomination in 2003, the press used this phrase—consistently out of context—as a snappy one-liner to try to portray Clark as a trigger-happy general.

Kosovo was NATO's first military engagement of its kind, and with no allied casualties it was a successful test of the organization's ability to play a significant role in the post–Cold War world. As the Serb forces pulled out of Kosovo for eleven days, NATO forces arrived to bring humanitarian relief and to help reduce the potential for a violent Albanian backlash against the retreating enemy. The refugees poured back into Kosovo from neighboring Albania, Montenegro, and Bosnia-Herzegovina in what was "the largest spontaneous return of refugees in Europe since World War II," wrote Clark in *Waging Modern War*. "We had our cease fire. NATO was there, and in charge, supporting the United Nations. This was success."[32] The conflict also confirmed the strength of modern airpower, which effectively prevented the need for troops on the ground.

Clark had successfully juggled the political, diplomatic, and strategic demands of his position, in spite of the difficulties he faced with his superiors. Europeans distinguished him as a leader who helped resolve a complex conflict that had threatened the stability of the entire region; his commendations included an honorary knighthood from Great Britain's Queen Elizabeth. Leaders at the Pentagon did not follow in kind, however. Rather than reward him with an extension of his three-year term, they cut his post short by three months. General Shelton called Clark one night in July 1999 to inform him of Secretary Cohen's decision to have him leave his command in April 2000. "SACEURs were expected to serve at least three full years," Clark wrote. "They are usually asked to extend for a fourth. But now, having just completed my second year at NATO, I was being told that my term would end in nine months."[33] It was shocking news, especially in light of the NATO victory and Cohen's earlier statement to Clark, in 1998, that he would have two more years in the job.

Shelton explained that it was all a matter of timing for

Joe Ralston, vice chairman of the Joint Chiefs, who was to replace him as SACEUR. According to army regulations, if Ralston did not have another post within sixty days of leaving his term as vice chairman, he would be demoted to two stars. His term was up at the Pentagon in February; therefore he needed to be sworn in as SACEUR in April at the latest. Two years earlier, Ralston had been passed up for promotion to chairman of the Joint Chiefs because of his admission that years earlier he had had an affair while separated from his wife. The SACEUR post was his last opportunity to remain in command.

That explanation "didn't wash," wrote Clark. "I was sure that legal arrangements could have been made to enable me to complete three full years."[34] Shelton cut the conversation short, and before Clark could collect himself enough to try to talk to someone else about the situation, he got a call from a *Washington Post* reporter who asked him to confirm that he would be replaced by Ralston in April. "Because his peers did not trust him," wrote Halberstam, "and did not want to give him any wiggle room (they feared he might use his Clinton connections to reverse their decision), they had leaked the story to the *Washington Post* that very night. . . . Rarely had the commanding general in a victorious cause been treated so harshly." Halberstam added that the Pentagon had described the transfer of command to Clinton as a routine, normal rotation rather than a forced retirement. "Clinton signed on, apparently not realizing that he had been snookered," he wrote. "Later Clinton was said to have been quite angry about what had happened," and Albright was also "furious about Clark's treatment."[35]

"I never saw myself as a fifty-five-year-old retired general," said Clark a few weeks after the announcement.[36] The Pentagon's low-key planning after the conflict revealed, to some, its desire to underplay the significance of Clinton's policy in the Balkans as well as Clark's victory. "The Pentagon, which refused to take the lead in the Kosovo peacekeeping operation, as it had done in Bosnia, put a one-star army general in command of the U.S. troops," wrote Dana Priest in *The Mission*. "To a remarkable degree, U.S. soldiers entering Kosovo would be left on their own to figure out the mission."[37]

In a commentary in the *Washington Post*, Patrick Pexton wrote that "Clark deserved more than a pink slip" for his command and described the stark contrast between his treatment and that of the generals who had commanded the war in Iraq:

> Nine years ago, Washington put on a lavish victory parade for the conquering troops of Desert Storm. The nation cheered the men and women who . . . defeated a ruthless dictator who had seized and pillaged a neighboring land. The generals who led an unwieldy multinational coalition to triumph were feted, toasted, and mentioned as presidential material.
>
> Not so for the general who won Kosovo, although he too ousted a murderous tyrant who burned and occupied a neighboring land. This general also led a cumbersome multinational coalition to victory in a short war—this time with zero combat deaths. . . . Clark's reward for victory is early retirement.[38]

Senator John McCain, the senior senator from Arizona who had been a navy pilot after graduating from the naval academy, issued a press release that described the repercussions this episode could have on future relationships between commanders and the White House:

General Wes Clark ably led NATO's campaign in
the Balkans. If his early departure is in any way
punishment for giving the Commander in Chief his
best advice and counsel regarding the dimensions
of our air campaign and the preparation for the possible use of ground forces, then I'm deeply concerned that this action will influence other senior
officers to place political considerations before military necessities and deprive future presidents of
the counsel they need to best protect our security.[39]

Clinton was vocal about his reaction to Clark's treatment as well, and told the press that he was "distressed"
by the way the public learned about Clark's replacement.
"Any inference that it amounts to an early retirement or
that somebody was disappointed in his performance is
just simply wrong. . . . I think Wes Clark's done a terrific
job. . . . I have great confidence in him, and his strength
and determination were very important to the outcome of
what happened not only in Kosovo, but earlier, his pivotal
role in the peace process coming out of Bosnia. . . . I have
the highest regard for him."[40] After Clark's retirement,
Clinton awarded him the Presidential Medal of Freedom
for his service to the United States.

Lt. Gen. Daniel W. Christman, who had worked with
Clark in the Joint Staff office and served as Super-
intendant of West Point while Clark was SACEUR,
explained one of the issues that fed the conflict between
Clark and the Pentagon and ultimately led to his early
retirement. The Joint Chiefs of Staff focused on potential
trouble spots all over the globe, such as Korea and the
Middle East, and in the view of some, Clark's insistence
on intervening in Kosovo came at the expense of other
concerns.

"Shelton and Cohen were looking at what they

viewed as the geo-political map," said Christman, "and Wes was single-mindedly focused on Europe. From where Wes was sitting, and I happen to think he was right, there was only one genocide occurring in the late 1990s [in the Balkans]. Both Wes and I were on the staff when the Rwanda genocide happened. We recoiled and said we cannot let this happen again. All of this played into some very sharp personality disputes, particularly when he took over the job as SACEUR."[41]

After the Serbian surrender, Clark's job shifted from war strategy to overseeing all the peacekeeping forces in Kosovo. Although Milosevic's forces had left Kosovo and the cease-fire was in place, it was still a dangerous region, as Clark discovered in March 2000. That month, the CIA uncovered a Serb plot to assassinate Clark and the new NATO Secretary General Lord George Robertson. Shortly before the pair were scheduled to fly via helicopter to Kosovo, the agents discovered that Serbs "intended to use shoulder-launched surface-to-air missiles to attack the chopper," according to the *Times* of London.[42] The trip itinerary was changed and Clark and Robertson made it safely to the Pristina airport.

After Clark completed his post, overseeing all the peacekeeping forces in Kosovo, Robertson praised him for his "military skill" and "real political acumen." He told Clark that he had contributed enormously to NATO and "helped turn the concept of a Euro-Atlantic community into a living reality. . . . Under the watchful eye of [NATO's Kosovo Force], a million Kosovars have returned to their homes and are now living in peace and freedom for the first time in a generation. [They] have at last achieved some real hope for the future. This is a historic achievement, and you have a right to feel proud of it." In his final address as SACEUR, Clark stated, "We have demonstrated that there is nothing stronger than the power of ideas—ideas of freedom, law and justice, and that democratic peoples united in vision of a common imperative form an irresistible and magnetic force which is transforming the very nature of Europe."[43]

Although Clark retired from the army in the spring of 2000, he was not finished with Milosevic. In December 2003 he was called to The Hague to testify at the former Yugoslav president's war crimes trial. Among the issues that the prosecutor asked Clark about was the Srebrenica massacre of 1995, when 7,000 Muslim men were killed by the Bosnian Serb Army. The trial was closed to the press, but Clark said that he was glad to have the opportunity to tell Milosevic's story. "For me, it was a very, very satisfying experience because I've watched the ravages of his leadership in Europe for years; I've seen the results in the shattered cities of former Yugoslavia." Milosevic, who served as his own lawyer, cross-examined Clark at the trial. This interaction "was a typical Milosevic performance," said Clark, "in which it was grandiose in effort, misplaced, in some ways overly personal."[44] Milosevic faced sixty-six charges at the trial—the most important war crimes trial since the Nazis were brought to justice at Nuremberg after World War II. Clark was the most senior official from the Clinton administration to testify. "It's precedent-setting," he said. "He's the first head of state to be tried by an international tribunal for war crimes and genocide. And participating in that trial gave me a first-hand impression of the benefits and of the complications of international tribunals."[45]

On his farewell visit to Kosovo in May 2000, Clark was pleased to see NATO's accomplishments in bringing humanity relief and peace to the province. "It was a great experience to come back and see what outstanding work has been done," he said. In his address, he emphasized the new direction that he hoped Kosovo would display to the world. "My message to them was that Kosovo has to belong to all the people who live here, not Albanians, not to Serbs," he said.[46] He knew that Milosevic's trial could last another two years, and trusted that justice would be done by the tribunal. In *Waging Modern War*, he stated that he "was proud that our country and our Alliance had learned, that we didn't 'turn our heads,' and that we hadn't stood aside to permit another tragedy in 1999 in Kosovo. And I was proud to have been part of that effort, even if it brought the end of my military service."[47]

SEVEN

★ ★ ★ ★

Boardroom Warrior

"It ain't so much trouble to get rich as it
is to tell when we have got rich."
—Josh Billings

In May 2000, Clark retired from thirty-four years of military service—thirty-eight including West Point. After nearly four decades of navigating clear-cut goals in the army, he began to carve out a new life plan at the age of fifty-five.

Thinking big had launched his military career back in high school, where he had announced he wanted to become a general. When the time came to make a new set of goals, he thought big again. Making money was a priority. Over the span of his army career Clark had only earned an average of $40,000 per year and, as the *New York Times* reported, he "left the military with precious little in the bank to show for years of public service."[1]

As a result, amassing wealth was number one in Clark's three-part plan for his new civilian life: (1) Enter the business world and accrue $40 million, which would enable him to become a philanthropist and support his pet interests and favorite causes; (2) become a university professor; and (3) roam the world's greens as a teaching golf pro. His golf handicap was eighteen in late 2003, and he considered the sport a challenge on more than one level. "Golf is like life," he said. "When you learn a sport, you go through the cycle of humility. You learn about yourself."[2]

Clark's inspiration for philanthropy came from his admiration of George Soros, the billionaire financier and philanthropist who gives hundreds of millions of dollars each year to several countries through his foundation, the Open Society Institute. His first effort in enhancing institutions and civil liberties throughout the world took place in South Africa in 1979, where he provided the funding for black students to attend the University of Cape Town.

Public speaking would become one of Clark's first business ventures and prove to be his most lucrative. Immediately upon leaving his post as SACEUR, he began jetting around the United States to deliver speeches about foreign policy, leadership, and the modern military to companies and organizations. Clark had grown accustomed to a large staff and a fleet of military aircraft to assist and transport him in Europe. Now, traveling around the country without so much as an assistant, the day-to-day details became almost comical. Flying over Arizona in a corporate jet to a scheduled appearance in the summer of 2000, for example, the crew asked Clark which airport, Scottsdale or Phoenix, would be closer to his destination. The general, who had just commanded a war for NATO, had no idea. The airports of the greater Phoenix area were not on his radar screen. "It's challenging without a staff," he admitted in those first weeks of civilian life.[3]

For advice on launching a business career, Clark turned to several former government officials who had successfully transferred to the private sector. One, Newt Gingrich, had found a new platform for his political interests as a senior fellow at the American Enterprise

Institute for Public Policy Research, a conservative think tank in Washington, DC.[4] Since resigning as Speaker of the House of Representatives in 1999, Gingrich had also written books and gone on the lecture circuit. His life was organized, Clark learned, by a publicist, an agent who managed his speaking engagements, and a nine-person staff set up in an office three blocks away from the White House. Striking out on one's own appeared to be an expensive undertaking.

Clark also sought the advice of Thomas F. McLarty III, a former chief of staff in the Clinton administration. "What you do when you're repotting yourself can be a tricky proposition," McLarty said. "Wes was gathering facts to decide what to do in the next passage of his life."[5] McLarty helped Clark focus on settling back in Little Rock to take advantage of his roots there.

Clark also spoke to his close associate from the Dayton period, Richard Holbrooke, who minced no words in spelling out the general's new status. "I told him, 'Trust me, no one has ever heard of you,'" said Holbrooke.[6] Clark protested that he had been supreme commander of NATO, but Holbrooke explained that he had not gained the visibility of Schwarzkopf or other warriors who had fought in Desert Storm. The war in Kosovo was not covered as extensively on television as the first war in Iraq was, and Clark was undoubtedly much more well-known in Europe than he was in the United States. In spite of that harsh dose of reality, Clark took McLarty's advice and resettled in his hometown, confident that he would be able to market himself in Little Rock's business community and beyond.

Hovering above the entire business community in Little Rock—and above the city itself, in the tallest glass building on the skyline—is the Stephens Group, one of the world's largest investment banks off Wall Street. Clark received entrée into Stephens through Vernon Weaver, a company executive who had been ambassador to the European Union when Clark was SACEUR. The United States Mission to the European Union is head- quartered in Belgium, which had put Weaver and Clark in close proximity both politically and geographically. Before receiving his ambassadorship, Weaver had worked for thirty-two years at Stephens Group, and he returned to Stephens after his departure from his post in Belgium.

His introduction was successful, and Clark joined the payroll at Stephens as a consultant in July 2000. Warren A. Stephens, president of the family-owned private firm, appeared at first to comply with Holbrooke's assessment of Clark. "Frankly, I did not know how he would fit in," Stephens said. "But he was a bright person and I thought, 'Let's see if he can bring in some deals.' Wes was able to open doors for us."[7]

As a consultant and later a managing director, Clark sought out technology companies that were looking for an investment partner. He preferred dealing with small entrepreneurial organizations, such as an electric propul- sion company in Virginia called WaveCrest Laboratories, and did not become associated with giant corporations like Boeing or Lockheed Martin as Generals Shalikashvili and Ralston, for example, had done. "Wesley Clark must be one of the few four-star generals not associated with a Fortune 500 company," said one military analyst in November 2003.[8] But Stephens Inc. is anything but small. By 1990, it had become the largest private investment bank in the United States outside New York. The company wielded a hefty influence on the national stage, and one author described it as Wall Street, on the River Arkansas.

The Stephens Group has a long history as a political power broker in Arkansas, funding campaigns of both Republicans and Democrats. Witt Stephens founded the company in 1933 and was joined by his brother, Jack, in 1946. Jack's son, Warren, became CEO of the company in 1986. Stephens is one of the biggest shareholders in multinationals throughout the world, including Arkansas-based corporations such as Tyson Foods and Wal-Mart. The bank played a major role in Wal-Mart's story, for example, as the underwriter of the retailer's first stock offering in 1970. One Arkansas journalist described the firm's private yet pervasive influence:

> For at least 30 years W. R. "Witt" Stephens and younger brother Jackson T. "Jack" Stephens, Warren's father, were the most powerful men in the state. Arkansas was their commercial and political fief, but most people never met or saw them, never heard them speak, seldom even saw their pictures in the paper and only rarely read a remark one or the other was said to have uttered. A savvy person could make out only the shadows of the brothers' unseen power: the governors, senators, congressmen, and state lawmakers whose elections the family helped bankroll, the laws that bore their stamp, the gas nearly everyone burned and that Stephens extracted and sold, the scores of schools and other public institutions across the state financed by Stephens-managed debt, the shopping centers, office buildings, and plants in which the Stephenses had a hand but which did not bear their name.[9]

Stephens' high-profile support includes the presidential campaigns of Jimmy Carter, both George Herbert Walker Bush and George Bush, and Bill Clinton. Clinton received substantial financing from Stephens at various times in his career; the company came through, for example, at crucial times in his gubernatorial reelection campaign and his first presidential campaign in 1992. Jack Stephens actually backed George H. W. Bush during the 1992 campaign, but a significant number of his employees supported Clinton. That year, "employees of Stephens Inc. gave more money to Clinton than employees of all but two other firms in the entire country."[10] As R. Emmett Tyrrell Jr. wrote in his Clinton biography, "The Stephenses had spotted Clinton for the political prodigy that he undoubtedly was."[11] Although the company has traditionally sought to make its deals out of the public eye, it has been thrust into the limelight from time to time with its association to headline-making events such as the campaign finance scandal of 1996. Jackson Stephens' business partner, John Huang, pleaded guilty to violating campaign finance laws after making phone calls to his former company, the Lippo Group, while he worked at the Commerce Department. The Chinese government owned a major portion of the Lippo Group, and Huang's frequent contact with the company raised red flags. He made his illegal phone calls from Stephens Inc.'s Washington office.

Clark's income jumped to six figures when he began his investment-banking career at the Stephens Group, where he worked directly for Jackson Stephens. A modest step toward his $40 million goal (a number he chose at random, simply to have a target in mind), his salary was soon augmented by big speaking fees. In late 2000, Clark signed on with the Greater Talent Network, Inc., the New York–based booking agency for public speakers. Holbrooke was also a client, and with Greater Talent's management, Clark's speaking career took off. The days of trying to figure out which airport to land in were over;

he would receive micromanaged treatment from one of the biggest agencies in the business. Clark discovered that he was in demand, which confirmed that he did have the star drawing power that he was confident he would have in the United States.

After the terrorist attacks on the United States on September 11, 2001, the demand for speakers who could talk about national security and foreign policy skyrocketed. Don Epstein, the president of Greater Talent Network, said that Clark became a top draw after 9/11 when the interests of the business community shifted. "Prior to September 11, a lot of business people out there wanted to know where technology was going," said Epstein. "And the political side of things was not so hot. Now, people are looking to talk about...how corporations do business in this foreign policy climate."[12] Clark addressed these interests with speeches such as "The Front Lines of International Economics," and it paid very well. In seven months of 2002 alone, he delivered fifty-five speeches for which he was paid $1.41 million, or approximately $25,000 per appearance.[13]

Clark's well-written speeches and eloquent delivery—his years as a competitive debater had laid the foundation for this career—brought him a heavy schedule of engagements at colleges, investment firms, businesses, and other venues. Typical trips on his globe-trotting speaking schedule included a Warner Home Video meeting in France, a series of speeches for Lehman Brothers at various locations, a speech for Deloitte-Touche in Venice, and a Forbes Conference in Lake Tahoe. In January 2003 he was one of the star speakers at the World Economic Forum's Annual Meeting in Davos, Switzerland, sharing the podium with Colin Powell, Jordan's King Hussein, and Brazil's President da Silva.

After setting up at Stephens, Clark joined the boards of several companies headquartered in Little Rock and elsewhere. His affiliation with Acxiom, a Little Rock company that creates and sells mailing lists as well as other data services, began after the attacks of 9/11. Acxiom, which claims to have information on 96 percent of U.S. households, discovered that they possessed personal information on eleven of the nineteen terrorist hijackers who struck that day. They hoped to turn that information, as well as their colossal database resources, into homeland security contracts with the government. Clark's first involvement with the company was in making phone calls, on a pro bono basis, to some high level Washington officials on their behalf. "He helped us for two or three months," said Acxiom CEO Charles Morgan, "calling and offering ideas, telling us what sort of services might be needed for the nation. I told him, 'You can't just keep doing this for free.'"[14]

In December, Morgan made a deal with Stephens to remedy that situation and to solidify his company's relationship with Clark. Acxiom signed a $300,000 contract with the Stephens Group, who set up a new subsidiary named SCL LLC, solely for aerospace and defense consulting. Clark was the only employee and Acxiom the only client.[15] Clark's portion of the $300,000 is unknown, but Acxiom also made him a member of their board of directors that same month. Morgan commented that one of Clark's motivations for joining Acxiom was his gung-ho attitude in the wake of the terrorist attacks. "Like all of us around 9/11, he had a lot of patriotic fervor about how we can save our country," he said.[16]

Clark had actually been invited to be on Acxiom's board the previous year, just as his retirement from the army was announced. Morgan had heard a lot of talk about Clark when he attended an international business roundtable in Brussels, Belgium, in early 2000. "When I arrived in Brussels, everyone was saying, 'We're so sad Wes Clark is leaving.' At that time, I'd forgotten he was from Arkansas. I was fascinated that Wes was so popular in Europe." Morgan was compelled to wonder, "Does this guy walk on some sort of water or what?" Later that year, when Morgan heard that Clark was retiring, he asked him to join the company, but Clark declined because he was still weighing his options. When Clark did start working for Acxiom in late 2001, he helped the executives get meetings with Vice President Dick Cheney, Transportation Secretary Norman Mineta, Human Services Secretary Tommy Thompson, and others.[17] "He's a bit of a technologist, and . . . we're about technology, so it seemed like a logical idea," Morgan said.[18] Clark joined the ranks of the defense-related lobbying industry when he became an official lobbyist for Acxiom in 2002.

In the wake of 9/11, privacy was a white-hot issue as the government sought out ways to identify terrorists. Acxiom came under fire for its participation in one of those efforts when a privacy rights group, the Electronic Privacy Information Center, filed a complaint with the Federal Trade Commission in January 2004. The group claimed that Acxiom did not adhere to its own privacy policy when selling information about two million JetBlue passengers to a government contractor, Torch Concepts. Acxiom's information included passengers' gender, incomes, number of children, Social Security numbers, occupations, and whether they owned their homes and how long they'd lived there. This data was used to develop an airline security project, and according to the privacy group, Acxiom was obligated to let the passengers know that their information was being used. Acxiom denied that it breached its policy, which, they said, provides personal information to "government agencies for the purposes of verifying information, employment screening, and assisting law enforcement."[19] Clark's work at Acxiom included "information transfers, airline security, and homeland security issues," but Acxiom spokesman, Dale Ingram, told the *Arkansas Democrat-Gazette* that Clark was not involved in the contract targeted by the privacy group.[20]

Clark and his wife had moved to Arlington, Virginia, when they returned to the United States from Belgium in 2000. As Clark's business opportunities in Little Rock expanded, he and Gert began looking for a house in his hometown. In March 2001 they bought a 4,023-square-foot home in the exclusive Robinwood subdivision for $459,000.[21] The neighborhood lies north of Reservoir Park and about eight miles west of Pulaski Heights, where Clark grew up. Clark's latest housing in Mons, Belgium, was a grandiose exception to the type of military housing he and his family had lived in for the bulk of his military career. Now, for the first time, he and Gert settled into their own place without another move looming on the horizon. They had moved thirty-one times in their military years, but now they could put down roots. Gert got involved in the city by joining boards, such as the Little Rock Boys and Girls Club, which had played a big part in her husband's childhood. "It's amazing," said Clark's second cousin Mary Campbell, "she came here as a stranger, not knowing anybody but family, and she's accomplished so many things. She's so adaptable."[22]

Another company that Clark advised as a banker at the Stephens Group was Silicon Energy Corp., a software maker for energy companies in Alameda, California.

Stephens owned stock in the company, which was trying to break into the government market. In addition to helping Silicon executives understand the federal procurement process, Clark provided them with contacts at the navy and air force and gave them some basic business advice. "I actually used him more for management questions," said John Woolard, the founder of Silicon. "He has a good head on his shoulders about how to work with people."[23]

As an adviser at Time Domain, a technology company in Huntsville, Alabama, Clark helped the company market a product described by *Business Week* as "X-Ray Vision for G.I. Joe."[24] Clark was introduced to the company by a Time Domain executive who had been a colonel under his command at NATO. He and other NATO personnel highly recommended Clark as a good fit with the company. "Everyone was saying, 'You guys need to have General Clark,'" said the company's CEO, Ralph Petroff.[25]

Time Domain was developing an ultra wideband, or UWB (a type of radar), technology for military use called SoldierVision. This technology allows users to see through walls and underground, and also enhances communications by making them less vulnerable to interception. Petroff explained that when pointing SoldierVision at a wall, "what you see is an outline of the room behind, with people showing up as yellow blobs." The unit focuses on large bags of salty water, "which is what human beings are," he said. Guns and other metallic objects show up as blue, so if a soldier sees a blue streak on a yellow blob, he can surmise it's someone carrying a weapon.[26] Time Domain is also working on a chip that can create an invisible shield around cell phones and other communication devices that makes them more secure—another high-tech advancement with a big potential for military applications.

The *Wall Street Journal* reported that Clark "counseled the company on how to answer Pentagon concerns that its low-power radar system might interfere with global positioning and communications systems, as well as to better craft that technology for military use."[27] Petroff described Clark's role as advisory only, stating that he did not act as a lobbyist for the company. "Wes was not going to the Pentagon and saying, 'Hey folks, buy a bunch.' His value was in pointing out what the military needs were and what would be of value to the soldier in the field."[28] He added that "few people in the military today have the perspective of General Clark, in terms of what the needs arc on the modern battlefield."[29]

Clark's board membership at Entrust, an Internet security company in Dallas, was also facilitated by someone he met during his army career. Entrust CEO William Conner and Clark had served together on an advisory panel at the Pentagon. Similar to his advisory role at Time Domain, Clark's work at Entrust involved exploring how the Internet security systems could be utilized by the government. In August 2002 he and Conner wrote an opinion piece that was published as a resource on the company Web site (and later as an opinion piece in the *Washington Times*). Excerpts from this piece warn about a potential terrorist battle tactic, to which the United States at its current level of technology is dangerously vulnerable:

> We are battling terrorism on all the traditional fronts—land, air, and sea. Yet we have begun to realize that, as in every war of the past century, advances in technology present us with new and vastly different fronts.

The next battle in the war on terrorism may be on the "cyber front." It offers relatively easy opportunities for our enemies given that our nation now vitally depends upon computer and network infrastructures that control everything from our electric power grids to financial institutions. . . . Yet our nation remains exceedingly exposed to cyber attack. America has moved neither fast enough nor far enough to secure these systems.

Are the terrorists capable of a cyber attack? It is abundantly clear from recent news stories that our enemies, including Al Qaeda, know how to use information technology to conduct covert communications (such as hiding messages in otherwise innocent pictures). News accounts also have shown that they have indeed targeted our critical infrastructures for attack.

We need to quickly devise and implement a national cyber security plan—a plan that is a partnership between the private and public sectors as mandated by President Bush.[30]

Another Internet security company, Presideo, Inc., invited Clark to its board in early 2001. Presideo, headquartered in Sebastian, Florida, specializes in protecting the confidentiality of health care information. "General Clark brings a wealth of intellectual and strategic resources that will allow Presideo to continue to develop and deploy superior security solutions to the health care industry in the U.S. and in European markets," said CEO Sheila Schweitzer. Clark said that he was impressed with the company's leading technology. "It's exciting to be working with an organization that solves real security issues that will ultimately protect the confidentiality of sensitive personal information while streamlining workflow, improving operating efficiencies and enabling improved patient care."[31]

While companies like Time Domain, Entrust, Presideo, and others were attracted to Clark for his technology savvy, others looked to different facets of his background. Messer Griesheim, an industrial gas supplier in Krefeld, Germany, brought the general onto their board for his "extensive European contacts," according to a spokesman for the New York investment firm Goldman Sachs, which partly owns the company.[32] Messer's products are used in several industries, from automobiles and electronics to pharmaceuticals and steel plants. Clark also joined the board of directors of SIRVA, Inc., the parent company of Allied Van Lines. This company hoped to benefit from Clark's military connections to enhance its business in moving military families. In 1999, Allied was the biggest moving company in the world and America's biggest armed forces mover, handling 20.9 percent of domestic moves for the military.

All of the firms Clark worked for were solid, successful businesses—with one exception. Cambrian Communications, a fiber-optics company in Fairfax, Virginia, owned an approximately 1,300-mile fiber-optic network along the East Coast and was named one of nine "Red Hot Startups" by *America's Network* magazine in 2001.[33] It was a star company when Clark joined the board in the summer of 2000, but in September 2002 it filed bankruptcy. The following year it was purchased by PPL Telcom, a utility company in Pennsylvania. The rise in wireless technology was one ingredient in the downfall of dozens of companies like Cambrian. In October 2002, an industry news source listed sixty-seven major fiber network, cable, and satellite company bankruptcies.[34]

Another factor was fiber-optic companies' early push to create expensive systems that the public was not ready to buy. An Associated Press reporter explained the paradox of the Internet boom: "Telecom companies laid down way too much fiber-optic cable, creating network capacity that won't get used for years, but failed to establish enough high-speed connections to individual homes."[35] Cambrian had offered Clark his first board of directors seat, but like other companies failed to survive in a fast-changing telecommunications industry.

With a career that involved policy research for the military, such as his J5 post in the 1990s, as well as hands-on experience with U.S. foreign policy in the Balkans, Clark was a good candidate for policy research institutes, or think tanks. He joined three of them during the first phase of his new life plan. At the Center for Strategic and International Studies (CSIS), he became a senior adviser, joining his friend, Thomas McLarty, who gave him advice when he was venturing into the business world. Sam Nunn, who served as a senator from Georgia for twenty-four years, is the chairman of the board of trustees, and the member level of CSIS includes past national security advisers Henry Kissinger, Zbigniew Brzezinski, and Brent Scowcroft. Based in Washington, DC, CSIS focuses on three areas of research: challenges to national and international security, expertise on all the world's geographical areas, and developing modern methods of governance through technology, energy, trade, finance, and public policy.

Clark also joined the International Crisis Group, headquartered in Brussels, which analyzes problems throughout the world in an attempt to "prevent and resolve deadly conflict."[36] Like CSIS, this group was guided by a distinguished board including George Soros, the philanthropist whom Clark admired and hoped to emulate with his own fortune one day.

The third think tank Clark joined was the Atlantic Council, which dates back to the years following the signing of the North Atlantic Treaty in 1949. The nonpartisan council was formed to enrich the public debate about critical international issues and to nurture future American leaders through educational and exchange programs. All of the activities of the council are "based on the conviction that a healthy transatlantic relationship is fundamental to progress in organizing a stronger international system."[37]

One of Clark's contributions was coauthorship of a policy paper entitled "Permanent Alliance? NATO's Prague Summit and Beyond." This paper came out of a working group that discussed NATO enlargement, NATO-Russia relations, the future of NATO in the Balkans, and other issues that would be discussed at the Atlantic Alliance in Prague in 2002. The report included recommendations about U.S. policy on these issues and was forwarded to Congress.[38]

Christopher Makins, the president of the Atlantic Council, expressed his appreciation for Clark's work in the Foreword of the policy paper: "First and foremost, we appreciate the intellectual leadership of Wesley Clark and Chas Freeman, who generously made a great deal of their time available to manage the group's meetings."[39] Freeman had been assistant secretary of defense for international security affairs from 1993 to 1994.

As soon as Clark retired in the summer of 2000 he began writing his first book, *Waging Modern War: Bosnia, Kosovo, and the Future of Combat.* This memoir gives a detailed look at his work in the Balkans, from his J5 days and the Dayton Peace Agreement to his role as SACEUR and fighting the NATO war in Kosovo. He also included brief autobiographical sections about growing up in Little Rock, attending West Point, fighting in Vietnam, and serving in various command posts throughout his career. A small, prominent New York publisher, PublicAffairs, part of the larger Perseus Books Group, released the book in 2001, and followed up with Clark's second book, *Winning Modern Wars*, two years later. This book, published during the campaign for the Democratic presidential nomination, examines the U.S. war strategy in Iraq and contains scathing indictments of the Bush administration's policies and war strategy.

In March 2003 Clark stepped down from his banking job at Stephens to form his own consulting company, Wesley K. Clark & Associates. "It was a very amicable parting, very comfortable," said a Stephens spokesman.[40] His client, Acxiom, came along after renegotiating the contract they had set up with Stephens. When asked about his company, Clark told the *New York Times*, "It's just general business services. We'll see where it goes."[41] During this period he was spending about one-fourth of his time working for WaveCrest and the rest serving on corporate boards and think tanks, and continuing to hit the airwaves as CNN's senior military analyst.

Since his hire at the network in 2002, Clark had become a familiar face as a regular commentator on military matters. Part of his reason for quitting Stephens was his anticipation that war was imminent and that he would be stepping up his work for CNN. "When the war starts, I'll probably be sent out there," he said, referring to a possible assignment in Kuwait. "It's just very busy right now and I felt like the time was right."[42] All the networks hired military analysts to comment on the brewing situation in Iraq, and an *Esquire* writer gave Clark the highest rating among them in a war pundit "charisma index": four-and-a-half stars out of five. "His words carry weight. Even Blitzer lets him talk," wrote Peter Martin.[43]

CNN was very lucrative; the *New York Times* reported that he made at least $1,000 per appearance, and his financial disclosure statement stated that he earned $490,000 from the network before his contract ended in May 2003.[44]

By the end of 2002, Clark had become a millionaire with an income of $1.7 million and assets totaling $3.1 million.[45] The majority of his salary had come from Stephens, although the company admits that he did not make any big deals during his years there. "It would be incorrect to say Wes made a big contribution while he was here, but it would be wrong to say we expected that, either," said Warren Stephens. He added that there were not "any significant dollars we could place by his name. . . . Wes certainly was helpful in opening doors, but that was about the extent of it."[46] The CEO also remarked that his privacy-conscious company was not pleased to be put in the limelight over Clark's run for the presidency. "Our company isn't looking to get into the spotlight," Stephens said, "and I'm not happy that it has been put upon us with Clark's candidacy."[47]

The two books Clark wrote were not a big source of income; he received a mid-five-figure advance for the first title in contrast to the million-dollar memoir deals signed by Gens. Colin Powell and Norman Schwarzkopf. "Our authors don't get rich on the front-end of our books," said Gene Taft of PublicAffairs, Clark's publishing house. Both of his books have gone back to press more than twice, however, and have done well for books "of their type," according to Taft.[48] When Acxiom brought their business over to Clark's new consulting firm, they paid him $150,000 per year plus expenses, in addition to board fees of $23,000[49] and $54,500 in company shares.[50] Each of his board memberships contributed to his income, with the exception of the International Crisis Group, which does not pay fees. He earned returns on his stock portfolio, and a significant amount of his income came from his speaking engagements.

In spite of what Holbrooke saw as the general's anonymity when starting out, Clark did very well in the first three years of civilian life. He said that he acquired his corporate posts "because I was a smart guy who could provide leadership."[51] A true technoid, he conducted his business with the help of an array of high-tech gadgets. "He's an incredible multi-tasker," said WaveCrest's Tom McMahon. "He carries two cell phones with him, a BlackBerry and a small handheld computer. He would sit at his desk, look at the company email, watch TV news, have a conference call going on with a corporate board all at the same time."[52] Clark's WaveCrest colleagues were also surprised by his low-key style when traveling from Little Rock to Washington. He flew coach, rented a small car to drive to their Dulles office, and always stayed at the Marriott in Arlington, Virginia, so he could get to the Pentagon swimming pool before 6:00 a.m.

Clark's new income by the year 2003 didn't put a big dent in his $40 million goal, but his three-point life plan had begun to shift by then anyway. A new track began to emerge as he witnessed changes in the country, changes that he passionately felt were driving the nation in the wrong direction. His notions of changing the world as a philanthropist gave way to serious consideration about running for public office, where he could work on problems from within the system. Problem solving has been one of his fortes since tackling his first math word problems at Pulaski Elementary, and finding solutions—whether in mathematics, physics, economics, military strategy, or diplomacy—is one of the most prominent skills in Clark's stockpile of talents.

EIGHT

✯ ✯ ✯ ✯

General Relativity

"We need a vision of how we're going to
move humanity ahead, and then we
need to harness science to do it."
—Wesley Clark[1]

Math has always been a breeze for Wes Clark. From
high school calculus to a course at the National War
College that explored the intricacies of the national
budget, Clark thrived on the left-brain challenges of
numerical, analytical thinking. Reading science fiction in
his youth fueled a passion for imagining the possibilities
that physics could unravel in the real world. This type of
thinking—envisioning beyond the borders—has intoxi-
cated Clark since childhood. His high school physics
classes were an invitation to ruminate on the future and
the subject continued to enthrall him in his classes at
West Point. "My physics teacher at West Point told me:
'Whenever I drop a piece of chalk I always look up,
because according to quantum physics there is always a
small chance that it will fly up. So if it happens I want to
see it.'"[2]

Clark is a self-described "scientifically inclined
[physics] wannabe."[3] On the campaign trail in September
2003, he revealed the full punch of his scientific mind-
frame to the public. At a party in New Hampshire, he
talked about the need for a strong commitment to high
technology in the United States, adding a flourish about

his own vision of human potential. "I still believe in e=mc², but I can't believe that in all of human history, we'll never ever be able to go beyond the speed of light to reach where we want to go. I happen to believe that mankind can do it. I've argued with physicists about it, I've argued with best friends about it. I just have to believe it. It's my only faith-based initiative."[4]

His joke on Bush policy got big laughs in the room and his topic elicited a string of humorous headlines around the world: "Spaceman Clark" in London's *Financial Times*, "Beam Us Up, General Clark" in the *New York Times*, "Clark Is Light-Years Ahead of the Competition" in the *Washington Post*, and "General Relativity (Retired)" on the *U.S. News and World Report* daily Web site. Although Clark didn't mention time travel in his comments, the subject of faster-than-light travel spurred reporters to link it with that subject. David Letterman joked on *Late Night* that Clark was already toying with the idea: "As a matter of fact, earlier today he went back in time to remove his foot from his mouth," he said.

Einstein's special theory of relativity carries a hypothetical basis for time travel, in that people traveling near the speed of light would, on their return to Earth, find that everyone had aged exponentially in their absence because for the space travelers, time had slowed down. To some scientists, time travel is a real possibility; to others, it is a crackpot flight of fancy. In response to Clark's remarks, one physicist appreciated the fact that the general brought the debate to a wider audience. Marc Millis, founder of NASA's Breakthrough Propulsion Physics Project, told the *U.S. News* Web site Science & Tech page: "I am quite surprised to see this subject brought up on the presidential campaign trail! Debating the faster-than-light question can be quite useful to physics.... Yes, faster-than-light still appears to be impossible, although numerous contrasting articles appear in respectable scientific journals. By asking such 'what-ifs,' deeper assessments of what we know and what we don't know are coming to light. And, how useful would it be if it turns out to be possible? Well, the implications are astronomical, literally."[5]

Clark is the quintessential "what-if" person, taking in all the variables and formulating a variety of outcomes. As a practical person, he is also interested in advancing a plan to test those outcomes. Nowhere, perhaps, has his passion for scientific musing and exploration been more borne out in his career than in his association with WaveCrest Laboratories, the technology company in Dulles, Virginia, that produces a new type of electric propulsion system. As discussed in the previous chapter, Clark worked with WaveCrest first as a consultant at the Stephens Group and later as WaveCrest's chairman of the board. Most of Clark's corporate affiliations after his retirement from the army involved technology, and a closer look at his association with WaveCrest offers an inside view of how he put his technological know-how to work for him in the private sector.

The electric motor developed by WaveCrest uses a computer microprocessor to control how much energy is being used. The small, circular unit is designed to fit near or in the wheels of a bicycle, car, or any other type of vehicle, and it can also be used to generate electricity for windmills and other energy systems. Clark was introduced to the company by a consultant who worked for WaveCrest and had ties to the Pentagon. He asked the management if they would like to meet Wes Clark. "I didn't know Wesley Clark at all," said WaveCrest's former president Joseph Z. Perry, "just his name from the Bosnia situation; I never sold directly to the military in my career."[6] The young company was a perfect fit for Clark, whose background in science and technology fueled an interest in alternative energy sources and high technology.

The first meeting of the minds between Clark and WaveCrest was informal but intense. "I remember that day very clearly," said Perry. "Our company was very small, we had this dream, and Wes said, 'I'd like to just come out and meet the engineers and have you guys explain what you're doing.' So people sat around on the floor and we had pizza and a couple of beers and did equations on the whiteboard. And Wes was at home. He immediately connected with the science and the engineers."[7]

Allen Andersson, the principal investor and co-founder of WaveCrest, was astonished at the mathematical prowess and quick grasp of the new technology that Clark exhibited during that first meeting. "When it came to explaining what our company was doing, he understood it a lot better than I did," Andersson said. "He thought that I was just being modest; but no, he understood it and I didn't. I felt embarrassed because he went to West Point and learned how to march while I went to MIT and learned mathematics. He's a guy that does all the practical things, he knows how to move vehicles from one place to another and make sure they have good drivers and fuel and the right number of rest stops; but he's also right there on the theoretical science end of it."[8]

The talk that day was of electromagnetic cores, battery chemistries, algorithms, power-to-energy ratios, and electric drivelines. Not only were the subjects perfectly suited to Clark's background as an engineering major and military technology expert, the personnel at the meeting offered an interesting connection, too. This unique type of electric motor was the dream child of two Russian scientists who left their country after the breakup of the Soviet Union. One of them, Boris A. Maslov, had worked for the Soviet defense industry during the Cold War. Now, the new relationship between the former Soviet Union and the United States was playing out on a smaller scale between two men who had forged their careers on opposite sides of the Iron Curtain. Clark, who had studied Russian even before learning of his own Russian heritage, found himself in yet another new Russian-related situation, talking physics over beer and pizza on the floor at WaveCrest Labs.

Maslov holds a Ph.D. in electric and electronics engineering and had worked for the Moscow Institute of Physics and Technology, among other organizations, before founding his own business, the Electronics and Software Company. This firm was the first privately owned corporation to appear in Russia after the fall of communism. He left Russia for the United States in 1993 and founded an investment advisory company in Virginia, GlobalGate LLC. For several years Maslov corresponded with another Russian émigré, Dr. Alexander V. Pyntikov, a medical doctor from Belorussia who had also stepped into private enterprise in the new Russia. A prolific inventor with forty patents to his credit, Pyntikov developed a new field in which he applied his medical background with electronics, electric transportation, and computer programming. The research he had done on the brain and nervous system he now applied to engineering principles to break new ground in electric motor technology. "All my inventions are based on the human neural system," he explained.[9]

The two Russian inventors developed a breakthrough concept which would come to be known as the

Adaptive® system. Pyntikov moved to the United States in 1997, where he joined with Maslov and others to fine-tune their motor system and develop other projects. The patent for their motor was filed in 1998, and one year later they teamed up with Allen Andersson, the technology entrepreneur in Washington, DC, to launch WaveCrest Laboratories.

One of the first members of the new company was Joe Perry, a physicist with extensive experience in the computer industry and in corporate technology marketing. After graduating with a B.S. in physics from Duquesne University in Pittsburgh, Perry worked as an engineer developing nuclear power systems for Westinghouse. He was then recruited by Nuclear Fuel Services to work on developing nuclear reactor fuel at their labs in Maryland. He branched into telecommunications as an executive for Sperry Univac before veering into the computer industry, where he worked for CCI and RDI Computer Corporation. He then helped found Uniprise, which designed systems management products, and was its president and chief executive officer. Later, he combined all of his experience to form a consulting company, in which he helped small tech companies turn their ideas into products. WaveCrest brought Perry into the fold to help them break into the high-tech energy and transportation industry.

The group met Wesley Clark early in the formation of the company, but the timing wasn't right for a relationship with the Stephens Group. "It was early for us in the investment bank I was with to invest in this," explained Clark. "We knew it was several years away, yet the technology was incredibly promising. So I stayed engaged with the company and we consulted with them from time to time."[10]

In 2003, Clark spoke about WaveCrest's motor as a potential source for windmill energy when he discussed alternative energy sources during his campaign for the Democratic nomination for president. As Perry explained, "Wes is a big fan of this technology; I know he's mentioned it a couple of times on his campaign, which surprised me, when talking about how we need to put more emphasis in the United States on wind power. WaveCrest technology can be used to generate electricity, such as in electric windmill generators. Our products can do well with anything that moves."[11]

A unique aspect of the design is the motor's ability to determine how much energy is needed from one moment to the next. The computer within the motor makes those adjustments. "Our motors tend to have enormous power when you're going very slowly," explained Perry. "When you start moving you need a lot of power to get going, but then once you're moving it takes less power."[12]

As a result of its innovative, patented design, the electric motor always runs at peak efficiency. The company installed their system in a prototype car in late 2003 and introduced it to the industry. The batteries and computer elements were tucked into the trunk, and the motors were encased within the wheels. According to WaveCrest, the car of the future runs not on an engine and a transmission, but on a microprocessor, batteries, and small electric motors in the wheels.

Clark discussed with WaveCrest the advantages that the military could find in their motor system. "One of Wes's interests in talking to us was the fact that an electric motor is more efficient in battlefield operations than an internal combustion engine," said Perry. "For instance, he talked about how much oil had to be moved to keep the divisions moving in Iraq—hundreds of thousands of gallons a day. It's a huge logistics problem. The electric technology that the military is looking for is all geared to providing higher performance and greater fuel efficiency, because electric propulsion delivers more power for the energy used, and thus is more efficient."[13]

Another element that is particularly important to military vehicles is the motor's ability to stay cool and not be detected by heat-seeking technology. "Our motors do not waste energy," Perry said, "so they don't have big infrared heat signatures; therefore, they're not as visible to enemy observers or enemy missiles."[14]

Clark was very interested in the patents of the operation and took what Perry described as "a very militaristic view" of how to develop them. He suggested putting together "red teams" like those in military exercises, hiring outside firms to try to design around the patents just as the red team would try to outmaneuver the original proposal. "In the military, he explained to us, when you want to test the validity of an idea, you appoint a red team that will try to defeat the plan," said Allen Andersson. The red team will try to find a way around it that could overcome it, poke a hole in it. And he wanted us to put together red teams for all our ideas. He was, of course, used to having nearly 100,000 people working for him, including 100 in his house, when he was NATO commander. And I don't think at first he was entirely aware of our limited finances and human resources, but that understanding came soon enough."[15]

Clark would learn about more of the differences between running things in the military and in the private sector on the job after joining WaveCrest as chairman of the board in April 2003. The company's interest in Clark was not, contrary to much of the reporting during the campaign, motivated exclusively by his Pentagon connections. "I see it in the press all the time," said Perry, "that WaveCrest has Wes getting government contracts for us. There's nothing further from the truth. His mission wasn't to go down to the Pentagon three times a week and drag some multi-billion dollar order our way. We used him for all his strengths: his technology strengths, his leadership strengths, his inspiration to us, and for the fact that he was a luminary with a name that brought us attention. Frankly, we were an early-stage development company at that time and that wasn't what the Pentagon was looking for. When we got to the point where we were building real product, I told Wes that we needed a colonel-level guy who can go to the Pentagon or to the independent agencies, someone with enough stripes on his shoulders to know the protocol and who can present us well."[16] Clark recommended Michael Mehaffey, a retired colonel who had worked with him when he was J5 at the Pentagon. Mehaffey now runs the direct military programs at WaveCrest.

"We brought Clark on as chairman to provide overall guidance and to help us recruit senior-level people into the organization," said Perry. "He was very good in helping us bring on board our current management team because he's a name and we're a little company. As a result, we have an incredible record of hiring people." One example of the level of auto industry people Wes helped bring to the company is Richard Schaum, WaveCrest's vice president and general manager of vehicle systems. "We would go out to Chrysler to hire the head of product engineering, a man with 10,000 employees at Chrysler," said Perry. "Schaum's initial impression was, 'You're a hundred-person company, why would I bother?' But when he learned that Wes was here he took a closer look. Wes was instrumental in helping us bring those type of management people on board."[17]

Clark's recognition in Europe as the former SACEUR also opened doors for the company. "Wes could pick up the phone and call the president of BMW or the president of Mercedes," said Perry, " and in two seconds he's got them on the phone. He would say, 'I'd like you to send some technical people to look at what I've got,' and they would come to Loudoun County, Virginia. He's an icon over there."[18]

In addition to making introductions to foreign businesses and finding top-level executives for WaveCrest, Clark worked on company strategy, found strategic partners, made banking relationships, and helped the company get national publicity with segments on CNN, the Discovery Channel, and TechTV. He also represented WaveCrest at industry conventions and in marketing campaigns. He has been photographed, for example, demonstrating the TidalForce electric bicycle that has been sold to police forces and special operations units in the military.

The bike goes up to 30 miles per hour—Lance Armstrong speed, the company calls it—and looks like a mountain bike with a small motor mounted within the rear wheel. The motor runs very quietly, combining speed with stealth, and has other characteristics that fit the military. "Folded, it fits very easily in the back of a Humvee," said one company representative. "It also can be airdropped. A paratrooper can jump with it."[19]

Although the WaveCrest motor's first applications have been with high-performance bikes, the system is designed to work in wheelchairs, buses, trains, ships, and large military vehicles. The big goal, however, is to rule the roads all over the planet. "The real target is the automotive industry," said Clark. "This is the motor Detroit has been looking for."[20]

Perry remarked that Clark had a down-to-earth relationship with everyone at the company. "He would walk around the building and talk to the janitor and the people running the switchboard; everybody was equally important to him. He has that genuine connection that only a few people could make." Apart from the connections and the global fame, Clark was a source of inspiration for the management, the engineers, and other employees because of his enthusiasm for the products and his belief in their place in the country's future. According to Perry and other officers of the company, Clark had the ability to rally everyone and make morale soar. "Wes was really, in many respects, an inspirational leader," said Perry.[21]

In his comments upon being made chairman of the board, Clark pointed out big-picture impact of the alternative energy that WaveCrest proposed. "I believe this technology will make WaveCrest motors the propulsion of choice for the twenty-first century, leading to a new generation of vehicles with superior operating characteristics and creating a legacy of environmental responsibility."[22] If the movement of some Detroit auto executives is any indication, Clark appears to be right about the future of the electric car.

Gradually, the industry is recognizing the impact that hybrid (part gasoline engine/part electric motor) cars are having on a U.S. marketplace that is becoming more concerned with global warming and the auto emissions that contribute to it. As former Chrysler executive Richard Schaum stated when he joined WaveCrest, "I'm becoming a tree hugger."[23] Former Chrysler chief Lee Iacocca is also leaning in this direction as the head of EV Global

Motors, a company that makes electric bikes. If the transformation from combustion engines to electric motors does proceed in the automobile industry, the change will be phased and gradual.

Clark has learned firsthand about the challenges of incorporating this type of new technology to the existing manufacturing infrastructure. "I would like to see us improve the efficiency of our vehicles," he told EVworld.com. "It's when you get down to the practical aspects of how you do that that people have concerns about. Is it doubling the price of gasoline through a fuel tax? People don't want that. Is it driving them away from the kinds of off-road mobility and the larger, more comfortable vehicles they seek? People don't want that. What we're offering at WaveCrest is we'll put the fun in driving, and we'll do it in an environmentally friendly and a fuel-efficient way with this technology."[24]

The need for major federal investment in technology, research, and development, and a revitalized space program came up frequently in Clark's campaign speeches. "[We must] work on science and technology with a real national goals program that invests real money," he said in November 2003.[25] During a live online chat for the *Washington Post* that same month, he offered a "what if" about high-tech, eco-friendly exports: "We should be using grants and tax expenditures to insure that we retain or gain leadership in a broad range of technologies. I am especially interested in energy and ecology tech which could not only help us gain energy independence but also make us world leaders and major exporters in these areas. What if we could rival the value of oil exports from the Mideast with our own energy tech exports?"[26]

In the "Protecting the Environment" issue paper on his campaign Web site, Clark offers several plans for

Wesley K. Clark: A Biography

developing clean energy and reducing global warming,
each of which tie into his experience at WaveCrest. "This
nation can no longer defer serious action to reduce our
consumption of fossil fuels," he wrote. "We urgently
need to confront the challenge of developing a 21st century energy policy, both as a matter of national security—
to reduce our dependence on foreign oil—and to combat
the profound danger of global warming. This is a challenge that we can meet with American ingenuity, resolve,
and technological leadership." The twelve actions presented to meet this challenge included advancing "the
use of fuel-efficient cars, SUVs, and minivans . . . acceler-
ating the use of hybrid vehicles . . . [and] aggressively
[promoting] the use of renewable energy like solar and
wind. . . ."[27]

At the same function in New Hampshire in which he
talked about mankind traveling faster than the speed of
light, Clark spoke at length about his support of NASA
and the space program. Jay Bucky, M.D., an astronaut
who had conducted Spacelab research on a Space Shuttle
Columbia mission in 1998, asked Clark about his thoughts
on the future of NASA. "America needs a dream and a
space program," he answered. "I was always a believer in
the space program."[28] He proposed that the nation make
clear goals and develop the technology to meet those
goals using a strategy similar to the military's Concept
Based Requirement System. When the military defined a
goal to keep tabs on the Soviet Union, it developed spy
satellites to achieve that goal. Clark suggested that the
space program would benefit from the same approach.
He then spoke about space exploration and his vision of
other high-tech advancements in the country's future:

I am a believer in the exploration of space. I'd like

to see mankind get off this planet. I'd like to know what's out there beyond the solar system. And I think that we need to make a deliberate effort to build public support for exploration of a new frontier. . . . There's probably nothing out there as dramatic as what John Kennedy did to reach the moon in eight years. But there are important goals that may take a lifetime to reach. We need to set those goals now. We need to rededicate ourselves to science and engineering and technology in this country. And by technology I don't just mean the Internet. I mean real technology across the spectrum of the sciences, the physical sciences, and the life sciences. . . . We need to look at extending the human lifetime so we can have better quality in our lives. We need to be able to investigate nanotechnology and really put that to work for us. And we need to look at the realms of applied and higher mathematics.[29]

Clark, who grew up during the space race and was inspired by President Kennedy's goals for man in space, has clearly retained his childhood curiosity about NASA and the science behind new technology.

After Clark announced he was running for the Democratic nomination in September 2003, his campaign officers advised him to step down from all of his corporate positions, including his chairmanship of WaveCrest. Although there is no law stating that a candidate cannot have a job during the campaign, contenders have traditionally left their positions because of the time and energy demands of campaigning as well as to avoid any conflict-of-interest issues. (Candidates who already hold public office, of course, do not resign their senate or governor's seat but keep collecting a paycheck even though their staffs take up a large portion of their workload.)

Clark's colleagues at WaveCrest knew it was coming. He had been ruminating about the run for months, and his mounting frustration over the Bush administration's terrorism and Iraq policy competed for his attention at work. "Towards the end he was becoming really distracted," said Joe Perry. "It was one thing to read in the papers about the rumors of him entering the race, but it was another thing to sit in the next office to him and see what was going on. You could just see that it was tearing him up; he just thought that what we were doing was bad for the country." To his coworkers, Clark's ambition was not about politics but about problem solving. In their day-to-day talks with him about the war on terrorism and the Bush administration's environmental policies, they witnessed a genuine concern that was personal. "You read that he's just another politician," said Perry. "He's kind of everything but."[30]

NINE

✯ ✯ ✯ ✯

"Welcome to the Party"

"I've always liked the battle of ideas."
—Wesley Clark, July 2003

At about the same time that George W. Bush was planning his transition to the White House in 2000, Clark was trying to determine where his politics would lie after retiring from the army. During the Bush-Gore presidential race, Clark evaluated the foreign policy platform of the would-be Bush administration and was not impressed. He had been selected to run the European command because he embraced the Clinton and Albright philosophy of interventionism on behalf of humanitarian causes, and no policy was more remote from this than Bush's evolving brand of national security.

Clark discussed this issue with Condoleezza Rice, Bush's campaign adviser and future national security adviser, while Bush was campaigning for president. According to Rice, the war in Kosovo would never have happened in a George W. Bush administration. A staunch adherent to *realpolitik*, or power politics, Rice was helping shape Bush's hands-off foreign policy ideas. National security, according to the power politics approach, is best served by confining the nation's diplomatic and military resources to conflicts that directly affect the nation's economic and political security. Using these resources to combat genocide, as was the case in Kosovo, does not fit into this strategy. To Clark, this was a sign that American

policy was "starting to go wrong" (should Bush win the
election).[1] He described his conversation with Rice as a
turning point that helped him form his own priorities
regarding America's role in the world:

> [Rice] told me she believed that American troops
> shouldn't be keeping the peace—they were the
> only ones who could kill people and conquer coun-
> tries, and that's what they should be focused on
> doing. What she was telling me [was] that she, as a
> potential Republican national security adviser, did-
> n't support our engagement in Europe. So I saw it
> going wrong from there. Then, as the administra-
> tion took office, I saw more and more what I
> believed were misunderstandings and missed
> opportunities.[2]

Not only did Clark disagree with the Bush camp on
an isolated foreign policy approach; he felt compelled to
do something about it. His fixation with the policies of
the new administration was coupled with a drive to take
action, just as his concerns about *Sputnik* and the
Communist threat had prompted him to learn Russian
and study rocket science when he was in grammar school.
Back then he had wanted to make a difference, to be part
of the solution, and this motivation proved to be a constant throughout his life. As a fifty-five-year-old, newly
retired general in 2000, Clark was unhappy with the state
of the nation and became even more disillusioned with
the Bush administration after the terrorist attacks of
September 2001. He agreed with Bush's strategy to try to
drive out Osama bin Laden with military strikes in
Afghanistan, but once the war effort turned to Iraq, Clark
no longer supported Bush's approach.

In November 2002, Clark met privately with a group
of affluent New York Democrats to tell them that he was

seriously considering running for president. Alan J. Patricof, the financier and chairman of Patricof & Company Ventures who had supported Al Gore during the 2000 campaign, hosted the lunch meeting at his Park Avenue offices.[3] He would eventually meet with all the Democratic contenders and choose to back Clark.

Clark voted for Al Gore in 2000 but had previously voted for Republicans, including Ronald Reagan in 1980. For many years he was a registered Independent, and during his campaign he explained that "in the armed forces you don't get into partisan politics"; regardless of the president's party affiliation, he is the commander in chief at the top of the military command. This nonpartisan look at leadership is reflected in his study of the nation's leaders—"I've always read about presidents"— and in his seemingly equal esteem for Republican Dwight Eisenhower and Democrat Harry Truman.[4]

"When it came time to choosing a party," he said, "I was pro-affirmative action, I was pro-choice, I was pro-education . . . I'm pro-health care. . . . I realized I was either going to be the loneliest Republican in America or I was going to be a happy Democrat."[5] He was attracted to the Democratic party because he liked "what it stands for," including "internationalism," "ordinary men and women," and "fair play."[6]

In the spring of 2003, a few months after Clark's meeting with Democrats in New York, his potential candidacy took on a life of its own with the launch of a grassroots movement called DraftWesleyClark.com. The organization was founded by John Hlinko, a thirty-six-year-old dotcom marketing director and political consultant who had developed his Internet savvy in his previous Silicon Valley career. On April 9, he sent an email to his brother-in-law, Josh Margulies, about his new Internet

project to drum up national support for Clark and ultimately convince the general to run. Margulies, a thirty-
three-year-old Republican lawyer in New York, was a
Republican who rarely agreed with Hlinko on these matters. He was shocked to get his brother-in-law's message,
because he had just launched his own site, Republicans
for Clark. They teamed up to bring their "guerrilla marketing" strategies to DraftWesleyClark.com and brought
in additional tech wizards such as Eric Carbone, a thirty-
three-year-old Internet entrepreneur who had already
retired after selling his company to AOL Time Warner.[7]

This group represented a new segment of society
that knew the power of the Internet and had the time
and money to put it to work for them. Their pioneering
work during the 2004 campaign was nothing less than
revolutionary, and changed the way Americans participate in politics. "A whole generation of highly skilled,
well-educated, entrepreneurial men and women" lost
their jobs after the stock market peaked in March 2000
and collapsed after 9/11, according to a profile of
Internet campaigns in the *American Prospect.* These affluent, unemployed products of the Internet boom formed
a "new base of wealth free from long-standing alle-
giances or deep involvement in traditional political circles," and were "steeped in the boom years' free-agent,
entrepreneurial, startup mentality."[8]

This combination of skills and wealth enabled people
like Hlinko and Margulies to turn their political ideas into
viable fund-raising and publicity machines. They produced radio and television commercials touting Clark's
military career and launched a system to collect signatures
requesting that Clark enter the race. Between mid-April
and mid-September 2003, DraftWesleyClark.com signed
up tens of thousands of volunteers, opened up a head-

quarters two blocks away from the White House, made 150 media appearances to talk about Clark, and raised $1.5 million in pledges for his campaign.[9] The purpose of this and other draft campaigns was to show the potential candidate an upswell of support and encourage him to run.

Democratic candidate Howard Dean and others had already discovered the power of the Internet as a campaign tool. For the first time, the grassroots movement was empowered by local get-togethers called Meetups, organized online, and a new form of lively commentary and feedback called Weblogs, or blogs. "In the modern age, the technology that is driving how people communicate at the front end of the campaign is the Internet," said Stirling Newberry of TheClarkSphere.com, another Clark grassroots site.

The organization that first informed Clark about his grassroots support was DraftClark2004.com, which presented him in May 2003 with 1,000 emails from people throughout the United States who stated that they wanted him to join the race. Founded by Susan Putney of New Hampshire, Brent Blackaby of California, John Oeffinger of Texas, and Jason McIntosh of Oklahoma, this group was the first Clark organization to file as a Political Action Committee (PAC) with the Federal Election Commission with the intent of persuading Clark to run for the nomination.

"Just fifty-two years ago citizens from all over the country were successful in their efforts to draft General Eisenhower," said Blackaby in June. "We intend to do the same in 2004 by drafting General Clark. If he runs, he wins."[10] Putney, who volunteered in this group while working full-time as a regional manager for a communications company, helped build a strong national infrastructure consisting of 200 Clark coordinators in all fifty states. She set up an office in a storefront in Dover, New Hampshire, which for many weeks was the only Clark-related office with a telephone number that potential Clark supporters—and the international media—could call.

Gordon Suber, a lawyer and retired businessman from New York who volunteered for Clark throughout the campaign, moved to Dover for two months to man the phones in those early days of the draft movement. "I wanted to commit real time, I wanted to get this guy to run for president," he said. "Susan was happy to find me because she was about to lose her main staffperson and needed someone to sit in the office and answer the phone. Up until Labor Day, the only phone number you could find on the Internet was that office. People were calling from all over the world, and at one point CNN sent up a crew. Other than a few students from the University of New Hampshire who came in occasionally, I was the only one in the office during the day."[11]

Suber's volunteer work in both the draft and campaign phase of Clark's bid for the nomination was ignited by Clark's strong credentials, as it was for other volunteers throughout the country. Without meeting Clark, he decided to support him after reading biographical sketches on the Internet. When he learned that Clark had been first in his class at West Point, Suber made a connection that eventually led to a surprising link between himself and the general. "My father-in-law, William B. DeGraf, was first in his class at West Point 1950. When I saw Clark on *Meet the Press* in June 2003, I thought that I needed to look into this guy because I had always considered my father-in-law the strategic thinker. He's not a guy that just advocates military force; he understands the big picture. This is the way these guys think."[12] After Clark officially announced his candidacy and Suber began working on his campaign, he learned that Clark had served under DeGraf in Vietnam. Col. DeGraf had led the First Brigade of the First Infantry Division, and Clark was one of the thousands under his command.

While the national grassroots movement worked to draft Clark he was working at home on his own deliberations about getting into the race. Gert, whom Clark has described as "street smart," wasn't naive about the dark side of American politics and was reluctant to put her family under the scrutiny of a national campaign. "It was a family process," Gert said. "Initially I was not delighted about it because I knew it would do a lot to our private life. It had to be something very thought out. As a wife and a mother the thing you want most is to protect your family. And you can't do that in a public arena." She believed in her husband but was not convinced that a national campaign was worth the toll it would take on their lives. They would lose their privacy and every word her husband said in his thirty-four-year career would be analyzed as potential ammunition to be used against him. She struggled with the decision until her son made a statement that put everything into perspective for her.

Like his father, Wesley Jr. was committed to the big picture. He and his wife, Astrid, were expecting their first child, and were looking to the future. "We went to see our son out in California," said Gert. "I said, 'This will affect your life. Things will never be the same.' He said, 'That's OK, Mom, I think things have to change, and we're willing to do it. And I want my son to grow up in a different world.'" His belief in his father's ability to help shape that new world was the clincher for Gert. "That did it for me," she said.[13]

In June, Clark confirmed that the sweeping feedback from the grassroots organizations were having an effect on him. He appeared on NBC's *Meet the Press*, where Tim Russert asked him if he was running for the White House. "I'm going to have to seriously consider it," he said. "In many respects, I would like a chance to help this country."[14] The most well-known Democrat in the country also played a part in his decision. Clark told the *New York Times* that Bill Clinton encouraged him to run in 2003, and at a cocktail party the Clintons held at their home in Chappaqua, New York, in early September, Bill Clinton toasted Hillary and Clark as two "stars" of the party. Pundits speculated that the Clintons were maneuvering Clark into the race to be a "dark horse" for Hillary, shaking things up among the other candidates to clear a path for her to enter the race herself. This Clinton conspiracy theory was popular in the first months of Clark's campaign, springing from a frustrating lack of information about the extent of Clark's ties to Clinton.

On September 17, Clark announced his candidacy in Little Rock. He chose a site that represented one of his strongest childhood connections to the city. Standing in front of the Boys' and Girls' Club, surrounded by supporters and signs that read CLARK 04 and THE WES WING, he said, "My name is Wes Clark. I am from Little Rock, Arkansas, and I'm here to announce that I intend to seek the Presidency of the United States of America." He acknowledged the volunteers and organizations who had called for his draft: "This is a journey I couldn't begin without all of you, friends and family, high school classmates, business colleagues, close personal friends, from all over the state; especially I want to recognize the hundreds of people who are here because of the Draft Clark movement. Thank you."[15]

Clark brought together a staff that included several well-known members of the previous Clinton administration. Eli Segal, the campaign chairman, had been chief of staff of the Clinton-Gore campaign in 1992 and served as assistant to the president. Mickey Kantor, chairman of the steering committee, had been national chair of Clinton's 1992 campaign, secretary of commerce, and U.S. trade representative. Richard Sklar, Clark's chief operating officer, was formerly the U.S. ambassador to the United Nations, special representative to Bosnia for implementation of the Dayton Peace Agreement, and Clinton's special representative to southeast Europe, where he worked to promote the region's economic development. Clark's director of communications, Matt Bennett, had been deputy assistant to the president for intergovernmental affairs and had also worked on both the 1992 and 1996 Clinton-Gore campaigns.

Clark enlisted John Hlinko, of DraftWesleyClark.com, to continue the online campaign as the new director of Internet strategy, and the campaign took off with great fanfare by raising $3.5 million, or about $250,000 per day, in the first two weeks.[16] As the new face in a crowd of contenders, Clark received golden attention after his announcement, but the staff faced a tough challenge to organize in such a short time. "We weren't just off to a slow start, we stumbled on our knees as we were getting into the race," said Sklar. "We had to do in seven weeks what some people did in a year or eighteen months."[17]

"From the minute he announced the campaign," said Suber, "he had the four no's: no money, no political experience, no organization, and no position papers." But volunteers like Suber who had helped draw Clark into the race would be able to help with the organizational issues. "At least he had the makings of a national organization with volunteers in each state who had been set up through DraftClark2004.com," Suber said. "They started getting the word out and provided a network of contacts that the professional campaign people could use.[18] Suber chronicled the critical role that these volunteers held in the Clark draft movement and campaign in a manuscript entitled *The General Who Would be President: One Volunteer's Pilgrimage with Wesley K. Clark*, and also co-founded the Wesley Clark Society as a forum for continued discussion and education on the issues brought up in the campaign.

Donnie Fowler, a Clark adviser before the announcement, had quietly become his campaign manager and was butting heads with the Clinton-era power players who began to take over the day-to-day work of the campaign. A lawyer from South Carolina and son of former Democratic Party chairman Don Fowler, he quit in the second month of the campaign over disputes about the role of the Internet-based, draft-Clark supporters and the Washington staff. Fowler believed that the grassroots personnel were not being taken seriously enough. He was not replaced until December, when Paul Johnson, veteran manager of several successful Democratic campaigns, was named campaign manager.

The nine Democrats already in the race for the nomination were former Illinois Senator Carol Moseley Braun, former Vermont Governor Howard Dean, North Carolina Senator John Edwards, Representative Dick Gephardt of Missouri, Florida Senator Bob Graham, Massachusetts Senator John Kerry, Representative Dennis Kucinich of Ohio, Connecticut Senator Joseph Lieberman, and New York civil rights activist Reverend Al Sharpton.

Clark came in as a pro-choice, pro-affirmative action centrist candidate and developed a platform that called for repealing the Bush tax cuts for those who earn more than $200,000 per year and providing health care coverage for uninsured Americans by transforming the present system rather than by creating a new national health care program. He promoted an environmentally friendly energy program that included reversing Bush's scaled down rules of the Clean Air and Clean Water Act and a commitment to confronting the global warming issue by reducing greenhouse gases. He vowed to restructure the war on terrorism by restoring America's relationships with foreign countries, building a new global effort, reviewing the Patriot Act, and making a $100 billion investment in Homeland Security. Funding for this and other programs would come through a budget plan that saved $2.35 trillion over ten years by repealing the Bush tax cuts, sharing the expense of the Iraq war with other countries, and cutting government waste.

From the start, much of the rhetoric from Clark and other candidates centered on criticism of Bush, from his tax cuts for the wealthy to the war in Iraq. In his first debate with the Democrat contenders, Clark said, "We elected a president we thought was a compassionate conservative. Instead we got neither conservatism or compassion. We got a man who recklessly cut taxes. We got a man who recklessly took us into war with Iraq."[19] As a first-time campaigner, Clark learned that his intellectual style of considering an issue from every angle and ruminating on several alternatives would not serve him well in the sound-bite format of modern political rhetoric. Just one day after he announced his candidacy, Clark made a statement about the war in Iraq that would haunt him through the rest of the campaign. On an airplane, a journalist asked him if he would have voted for Bush's resolution to go to war, had he been in Congress. "At the time, I probably would have voted for it, but I think that's too simple a question," he answered. A moment later, he added, "I don't know if I would have or not. I've said it both ways because when you get into this, what happens is you have to put yourself in a position—on balance, I probably would have voted for it." He quickly called his press secretary, Mary Jacoby, over to help clarify his position. She said to Clark, "You said you would have voted for the resolution as leverage for a U.N.-based solution," and Clark answered, "Right, exactly."[20]

The headline that ran in the *New York Times* on September 19, "Clark Says He Would Have Voted for War," provided Clark's rivals with ammunition to portray him as a waffler on the issues. He would be forced to go on the defensive on this point for months, including in the second primary debate, where he stated: "I think it's really embarrassing that a group of candidates up here are working on changing the leadership in this country and can't get their own story straight. . . . I would have never voted for war. The war was an unnecessary war, it was an elective war, and it's been a huge strategic mistake for this country."[21]

Another early snag in the campaign was the question of Clark's loyalty to the Democratic party. He did not officially register as a Democrat until a few days after he had announced his run, and a story about his previous interest in joining the Republican Party made big news. While attending the economic conference at Davos, Switzerland, in January 2003, Clark had talked with Colorado Governor Bill Owens and University of Denver President Marc Holtzman. The two prominent Republicans reported that Clark told them, "I would have been a Republican if Karl Rove had returned my phone calls." Clark remarked later that it was a joke, but *New York Times* reporter Katharine Q. Seelye conjectured that Clark may have been irked by the Bush administration's failure to ask for his assistance after 9/11. Even if Clark did not actually try to call Rove (Bush's senior political adviser), "one possibility is that . . . General Clark had simply expected to be called upon for his military expertise in helping to shape the war against Iraq," Seelye wrote.[22]

If his Rove comment was just a joke, it fueled the prodding about his allegiance to the Democratic party that came from journalists and Democratic rivals through much of the campaign. His oft-quoted pro-Bush statements at a Republican Party dinner in Arkansas in early 2001 also added to the controversy. At the Pulaski County event, which occurred four months before the attacks of 9/11, he said, "I'm very glad we've got the great team in office, men like Colin Powell, Don Rumsfeld, Dick Cheney, Condoleezza Rice, Paul O'Neill—people I know very well—our president George W. Bush. We need them there, because we've got some tough challenges ahead in Europe."[23]

Al Sharpton diffused the argument (and stole the show) one evening when he turned to the general during Clark's first Democratic debate and said, "Welcome to the party. It's better to be a new Democrat that's a real Democrat than a lot of old Democrats up here that have been acting like Republicans all along."[24]

One of the most painful moments of the campaign was the publication of a comment about Clark by General Hugh Shelton, who had been chairman of the Joint Chiefs of Staff while Clark was SACEUR. In October, newspapers throughout the world carried the response Shelton made when asked what he thought about Clark as a presidential candidate: "I've known Wes for a long time. I will tell you the reason he came out of Europe early had to do with integrity and character issues, things that are very near and dear to my heart . . . I'll just say Wes won't get my vote."[25] Clark tried to contact Shelton to ask him to elaborate on these "character issues," but could not get a response.

Shelton never clarified his statement to Clark or reporters, and the ordeal proved to Clark that the difficult relationship he had experienced with some military leaders would not disappear after his retirement from the army. It also confirmed Gert Clark's worst fears about campaigning. Among Clark's many supporters who expressed outrage by the comment was New York Representative Charles Rangel, who accused Shelton of "character assassination."[26] Rangel was one of Clark's earliest supporters and helped spearhead his campaign in New York, including a rally in Harlem that spotlighted a coalition of black leadership standing behind the general. When he appeared on *The Late Show with David Letterman*, Clark was again asked about Shelton's remarks. "It's a smear, that's all it is," he told Letterman. "And it doesn't have anything to do with the military. It's the kind of stuff of politics."

Among the high points during Clark's weeks on the campaign trail was the birth of his grandson, Wes, on Christmas Day 2003. Clark had missed this event when his own son was born during his tour in Vietnam, and he and Gert flew to Los Angeles to be at the hospital when Astrid Clark gave birth. Five minutes after the baby was born, Clark was on the phone to his second cousin Mary Campbell in Little Rock. "He was crying," she recalled, "and saying, 'It's a boy! I'm a grandfather!'"[27]

When Clark launched his campaign in September

2003, polls showed that Democrats were enthusiastic about his potential to win against George W. Bush. This spark of excitement came through in a CNN/*USA Today*/Gallup poll of September 22 that showed voters favored Clark over President Bush, 49 percent to 46 percent. In that poll, Clark was number-one among the Democratic candidates with 22 percent of the votes; Dean was second with 13 percent. By the end of October, the CNN poll showed Dean slightly ahead of Clark, 16 percent to 15. A *Newsweek* poll resulted in the exact same figures for Dean and Clark on November 10, but on the eve of the Iowa caucus, which Clark chose to skip in order to focus his resources on New Hampshire, Dean took over the lead with 26 percent of the votes, 6 ahead of Clark. Dean's front-runner status was dashed with his loss in Iowa, and from that moment Kerry took his place at the top of the polls. Leading up to the New Hampshire primary of January 27, Clark was third in the CNN poll, 12 points behind Kerry and 7 behind Dean.

Clark's performances in the first primaries (after Iowa) kept him in the top tier of the candidates. He came in third in New Hampshire—in a virtual tie with his fellow southern candidate, John Edwards—first in Oklahoma (with Edwards a very close second), second in Arizona, and third in Tennessee. Throughout the campaign, he remarked that it was the best thing he had done in his life, from one-on-one meetings with voters to national audiences—including his lengthy spot on the Letterman show—to the excitement of the crowds on his True Grits tour throughout the South. In his kickoff speech of the tour at Little Rock on December 29, Clark talked about his southern relatives on his mother's side of the family and announced that at every stop they would be "serving grits to anyone who'll take s'em." In that

speech, he also set the tone of the tour with remarks
about his southern roots:

> As an army man, I spent three decades living on
> bases all over the world. But it's like they always say,
> you can take the man out of the South, but you can't
> take the South out of the man. So no matter where
> I lived, I was always a son of the South. I never
> stopped thinking like a southerner or acting like a
> southerner—and I never stopped eating like a
> southerner. And there's nothing a good southerner
> likes more than a nice, hot bowl of grits. . . .
>
> My grandparents worked hard every day in the
> lumber mills of Arkansas just to make ends meet.
> Today, our family is mostly scattered all over the
> South, from Texas to Oklahoma. It's a typical south-
> ern family. Always trying to get together on the hol-
> idays, but never quite making it.
>
> It really all comes down to one thing: This elec-
> tion is going to be won by someone who under-
> stands southern values. Someone who's a leader—
> not a politician. Someone who believes that we
> should always put America's interests over the spe-
> cial interests, and who's always held accountable for
> his actions. We need a higher standard of leader-
> ship. That's what's going to turn our country
> around.[28]

The True Grits tour was typical of the whirlwind
schedule Clark kept during the campaign. The first day
alone took him to four states: Louisiana, Alabama,
Mississippi, and Florida. Another giveaway that had
become common at Clark speeches and rallies was the
Clark bar, and campaign staffers learned early that in
spite of his penchant for fitness and his daily swim routine, the general has an obsession for Cheetos.
Eventually, his cousin Barry sent him a supply of a

healthier, low-fat variety that didn't shed orange dye all over his fingers.

Like all the candidates, Clark had a cadre of Hollywood celebrity endorsers including filmmaker Michael Moore, director Barry Levinson, actor Ted Danson, actress and longtime friend Mary Steenburgen, and Madonna, whose endorsement in December quickly made international headlines. She told CNN that Clark "has a good handle on foreign policy, I think he's good with people, and I think he has a heart and a conscious-ness. He's interested in spirituality . . . those things mean a lot to me."[29]

Clark's third-place standing in Tennessee, however, along with a distant third in Virginia on the same day, proved that he had lost the South. With only one win in the primaries thus far, he decided to accept the inevitable and drop out of the race on February 11.

In his announcement that he was stepping down, Clark described the campaign as a pinnacle event in his long career in public service: "For me, this race has been one of the most liberating experiences of my life. I've been able to talk about what I believe in and fight for it. You've given me the greatest gift a person can receive: the support to make that fight real."[30]

The Democratic strategy had always been about building up the Democrat cause and finding the candi-date who could win against President Bush. Clark com-mitted himself to that plan by immediately endorsing the front-runner, John Kerry, two days later, stating, "I'll do everything I can to make sure that George W. Bush does-n't get away with playing politics with national security. George Bush has compromised America's leadership around the world."[31]

Unlike his father, Wesley Jr. did not hide his frustration over the outcome of the primaries. In early February, he told reporters that the campaign had been "a really disillusioning experience." He regretted that the message of his father's commitment to the country had not been heard. "We sacrificed a hell of a lot for this country over thirty-four years. We lived in a damn trailer when I was a freshman in high school. We always did it because we really believed in this country." He described politics as "a dirty business" and criticized the press for not telling his father's story: "His stance on the issues or his qualifications for the job haven't been talked about at all," he said.[32]

In retrospect, Clark felt that one of the biggest mistakes of his campaign was in the decision to not run in the Iowa caucus. In that first battle, John Kerry routed Howard Dean and began to gain a strong momentum. By not taking part, Clark missed the opportunity to show his strength at one of the crucial junctions of the race. On the evening of his campaign farewell speech, he shook hands with a supporter who told him that he wished he would have run in Iowa. Clark said, "Yeah, I wish we had, too. Everything would have been different if we had."[33]

In whatever capacity Clark continues his life of public service—as an educator, philanthropist, or politician—he can be expected to retain the personal characteristics that appeared early in his life and remained in place throughout his academic and military years. His brilliant intellect, talent for communicating, natural leadership, and endless capacity for work will continue to support his genuine commitment to making America a better place for its citizens as well as a "less arrogant" and more cooperative member of the global community. He sees change as inevitable, both for a post-9/11 world and for individuals. The race for the Democratic presidential nomination of 2004 was one of the very few endeavors in Clark's life in which he did not come out on top. (Perhaps the other most glaring example, also at the national level, was his television appearance on *Jeopardy* in 1969 in which, according to his friends, he "bombed."[34]) But Clark's ongoing transformation from soldier to civilian is a process that he knows will bring new wisdom as well as surprises. As he stated in a 1981 *Washington Post Magazine* article, in which he was singled out as "among the best the army has to offer," change is inevitable and natural. "If you say that someone hasn't changed, then there's a good chance that person hasn't grown."[35]

The campaign was a life-changing experience, a rigorous initiation into national politics. Although this rite of passage did not lead to the presidency, it stretched his boundaries as an extemporaneous speaker and as a problem solver for the big issues. In his remarks about leaving the campaign, he told his supporters that they would see more of him. "Folks, this old soldier will not fade away. No, I'm just going to change my uniform and get out in the field and work. I'll be out in front. I'll be working the issues. I'll be supporting the candidates. I'll be doing all I can to contribute to building a new and better America."[36]

Like his father, Clark was not about to fade into the woodwork after a failed campaign. Benjamin Kanne went back to work after those alderman elections of 1927. He had been an exuberant, beloved figure in his corner of the world, and his life as well as his untimely death made lasting impressions that are still evident in his son. Clark had the emotional security to forge ahead without his father, to respect his natural curiosity and act upon it, and to demand much of himself. He learned early to make every day count because life may be short. He inherited his father's drive and capacity for work and, without knowing about his father's career for two decades, his commitment to public service. As the record shows, that commitment has made an indelible mark on the U.S. Army and helped end ethnic cleansing in central Europe. It is a commitment from an unabashedly optimistic warrior-intellectual who believes that his country is not only the world's greatest military force, "but also its greatest force for good."[37]

Wesley K. Clark: A Chronology

March 1939	Marriage of parents, Benjamin Kanne and Veneta Updegraff
Dec. 23, 1944	Born to Benjamin and Veneta Kanne in Chicago, Illinois
Dec. 6, 1948	Death of Benjamin Kanne
1949	Veneta and Wesley move to Little Rock, Arkansas
Nov. 20, 1954	Marriage of Veneta Kanne to Victor Clark
June 1962	Graduation from Hall High School in Little Rock
July 1962– June 1966	Cadet at United States Military Academy (West Point); graduates first in his class and is commissioned as 2nd Lieutenant in the U.S. Army
Oct. 1966– Aug. 1968	Rhodes scholar at Magdalen College, Oxford University; promoted to 1st Lieutenant (with entire West Point Class of 1966)
June 1967	Marriage to Gertrude Kingston

Aug. 1968– Oct. 1968	Armor Officer Basic Course, U.S. Army Armor School, Fort Knox, Kentucky
Oct. 1968– Dec. 1968	Ranger Course, U.S. Army Infantry School, Fort Benning, Georgia; promoted to Captain
Dec. 1968– May 1969	Company Commander, A Company, 4th Battalion, 68th Armor, 82d Airborne Division, Fort Riley, Kansas
May 1969– Jan. 1970	Assistant G3, HHC, 1st Infantry Division, Vietnam
Nov. 1969	Birth of Wesley Clark Jr.
Jan. 1970– Feb. 1970	Commanding Officer, A Company, 1st Battalion, 16th Infantry, 1st Infantry Division, Vietnam
Feb. 19, 1970	Wounded in action
May 1970– September 1970	Commander, C Company, 6th Battalion, 32d Armor Division, 194th Armored Brigade, Fort Knox, Kentucky
Oct. 1970– May 1971	Armor Officer Advanced Course, U.S. Army Armor School, Fort Knox, Kentucky
May 1971– July 1971	Staff Officer, Plans Group, Office, Special Assistant for the Modern Volunteer Army, Office of the Chief of Staff, U.S. Army, Washington, DC

July 1971– July 1974	Instructor, later Assistant Professor of Social Science, U.S. Military Academy, West Point, New York
Aug. 1974– June 1975	Student, U.S. Army Command and General Staff College, Fort Leavenworth, Kansas; promoted to Major
Aug. 1975– Aug. 1976	White House Fellow, Office of the Director of Management and Budget, Old Executive Office Building, Washington, DC
Aug. 1976– Aug. 1977	S-3 (Operations) Officer, 3d Battalion, 35th Armor, 1st Armored Division, U.S. Army Europe, Germany
Aug. 1977– Feb. 1978	S-3 (Operations) Officer, 3d Brigade, 1st Armored Division, U.S. Army Europe, Germany
Feb. 1978– June 1979	Assistant Executive Officer to the Supreme Allied Commander, Supreme Headquarters Allied Powers Europe, Brussels, Belgium; promoted to Lieutenant Colonel
Aug. 1979– Feb. 1980	Executive Officer, 1st Brigade, 4th Infantry Division (Mechanized), Fort Carson, Colorado
Feb. 1980– June 1982	Commander, 1st Battalion, 77th Armor, 4th Infantry Division, Fort Carson, Colorado

June 1982– June 1983	Student, National War College, Fort Lesley J. McNair, Washington, DC
July 1983– Sept. 1983	Chief, Plans Integration Division, Office of the Deputy Chief of Staff for Operations and Plans, U.S. Army, Washington, DC
Oct. 1983– July 1984	Chief, Army Studies Group, Office of the Chief of Staff, U.S. Army, Washington, DC; promoted to Colonel
Aug. 1984– Jan. 1986	Commander, Operations Group, National Training Center, Fort Irwin, California
May 1986	Death of Veneta Clark
Apr. 1986– Mar. 1988	Commander, 3d Brigade, 4th Infantry Division (Mechanized), Fort Carson, Colorado
Apr. 1988– Oct. 1989	Director, Battle Command Training Program, U.S. Army Command and General Staff College, Fort Leavenworth, Kansas; promoted to Brigadier General
Oct. 1989– Oct. 1991	Commanding General, National Training Center, Fort Irwin, California; promoted to Major General

Oct. 1991– Aug. 1992	Deputy Chief of Staff for Concepts, Doctrine, and Developments, U.S. Army Training and Doctrine Command, Fort Monroe, Virginia
Aug. 1992	Death of Victor Clark
Aug. 1992– Apr. 1994	Commanding General, 1st Cavalry Division, Fort Hood, Texas; promoted to Lieutenant General
Apr. 1994– June 1996	Director for Strategic Plans and Policy, J5, The Joint Staff, Washington, DC; promoted to General
Jun. 1996– July 1997	Commanding General, U.S. Southern Command, Quarry Heights, Panama
July 1997– May 2000	Supreme Allied Commander Europe, Supreme Headquarters Allied Powers Europe, Belgium
June 30, 2000	Official retirement date from U.S. Army; move to Arlington, Virginia
July 2000	Joins Stephens Group (Little Rock) as consultant; joins board of Cambrian Communications; signs on with Greater Talent Network, a speakers' agency; joins Center for Strategic and International Studies (CSIS); joins International Crisis Group
Jan. 2001	Joins board of Presideo, Inc.

March 2001	Buys house in Little Rock
May 2001	Joins board of SIRVA, Inc., Publishes *Waging Modern War*
Dec. 2001	Joins board of Acxiom Corp.
2002	Registered lobbyist for Acxiom Corp.
2002–May 2003	Senior Military Analyst for CNN
March 2003	Resigns from Stephens and forms Wesley K. Clark & Associates
April 2003	Chairman of the Board, WaveCrest
Sept. 17, 2003	Announces run for the Democratic nomination for presidential election of 2004
Oct. 2003	Publishes *Winning Modern Wars*
Dec. 25, 2003	Birth of grandson, Wesley Clark III
Jan. 27, 2004	Voted number 3 in New Hampshire primary
Feb. 3, 2004	Voted number 1 Oklahoma primary Voted number 2 Arizona primary
Feb. 10, 2004	Voted number 3 Tennessee primary
Feb. 11, 2004	Drops out of Democratic presidential race
Feb. 13, 2004	Endorses Senator John Kerry

APPENDIX II

★ ★ ★ ★

Awards

U.S. DECORATIONS AND BADGES

Defense Distinguished Service Medal with four Oak Leaf Clusters (5)
> For Bosnia service
> Joint Staff, end of tour
> For service at U.S. Southern Command
> For service as Commander of the Kosovo conflict
> For service as Supreme Allied Commander Europe

Distinguished Service Medal with Oak Leaf Cluster (2)
> 1st Cavalry Division
> Upon Retirement

Legion of Merit with three Oak Leaf Clusters (4)
> Supreme Headquarters Allied Powers Europe (SHAPE) 1979
> Department of the Army Staff 1983
> MJC 1986
> MJC 1991

Silver Star Medal

Bronze Star Medal with Oak Leaf Cluster

Purple Heart

Meritorious Service Medal with Oak Leaf Cluster

Army Commendation Medal with Oak Leaf Cluster

Combat Infantryman Badge

Parachutist Badge

Ranger Tab

PRESIDENTIAL MEDAL OF FREEDOM 2000 CITATION

Respected for his military expertise, keen intellect, and diplomatic skill, General Wesley Clark has distinguished himself as a soldier, scholar, and statesman. Graduating from West Point at the head of his class, he set a standard of excellence that has been his lifelong benchmark, whether serving in Vietnam; as a key negotiator of the Dayton Peace Accords; or as head of the U.S. European Command. As Supreme Allied Commander of the North Atlantic Treaty Organization, he led the 19-member alliance to a historic victory in Kosovo in NATO's longest and most difficult military campaign. For his outstanding leadership and dedicated service, General Clark has earned the respect and admiration of a grateful Nation.

FOREIGN AWARDS

Honorary Knight Commander of the Most Excellent Order of the British Empire (United Kingdom)
Commander of the Legion of Honor (France)
Grand Cross of the Order of Merit of the Federal Republic of Germany

Knight Grand Cross in the Order of Orange-Nassau,
  with Swords (Netherlands)
Grand Officer of the Order of Merit of the Republic of
  Italy
Grand Cross of the Medal of Military Merit (Portugal)
The Commander's Cross with Star of the Order of Merit
  of Republic of Poland
Grand Officer of the Order of Merit of the Grand
  Duchy of Luxembourg
Grand Medal of Military Merit (Spain)
The Grand Cordon of the Order of Leopold (Belgium)
Cross of Merit of the Minister of Defense First Class
  (Czech Republic)
Order of Merit of the Hungarian Republic
Commander's Cross, The Silver Order of Freedom of
  the Republic of Slovenia
Madarski Konnik Medal (Bulgaria)
Commemorative Medal of the Minister of Defence of
  the Slovak Republic First Class (Slovakia)
First Class Order of Lithuanian Grand Duke Gediminas
  (Lithuania)
Order of the Cross of the Eagle (Estonia)
The Skandeberg Medal (Albania)
Order of Merit of Morocco
Order of Merit of Argentina
The Grade of Prince Butmir w/Ribbon and Star
  (Croatia)
Military Service Cross of Canada

SOURCES

✹ ✹ ✹ ✹

ARTICLES

"Acxiom's Stake in Terror War Under Fire," *Arkansas Democrat-Gazette*, September 24, 2003.

"After Retirement, Clark Has Forged a Lucrative Career," *New York Times*, November 10, 2003.

"After the Army, Clark Signs Up as Businessman," *Arkansas Democrat-Gazette*, October 2, 2003.

"America Must Be Prepared to Fight on a New Battlefield: The Cyber Front," Entrust Resources, www.entrust.com/resources/newsletter/dec02/article3.htm.

"American Journal," C-Span, interview with Gertrude Clark, January 25, 2004.

"An Arkansas Alliance, and High-ranking Foes," *Boston Globe*, November 17, 2003.

"Are Old-time Telecoms Beyond Hope?" *Seattle Times*, October 28, 2002.

Arkansas Boys' State Web site, www.arklegion.homestead.com/Boys_State.html.

"Balkan Nights," *U.S. News and World Report*, April 5, 1999.

"Banker Runs Off to Join the (Media) Circus," *New York Times*, March 9, 2003.

"Battalion Commander," *Washington Post Magazine*, May 10, 1981.

"Bike Boffins Pedal with General Clark," *Moscow Times*, September 23, 2003.

"Boy from Little Rock Chooses Military Path," *Boston Globe*, November 16, 2003.

"Boys' Club Campers to Attend U.S. Academies," *Arkansas Democrat-Gazette*, June 20, 1962.

"Cadet Clark Gets Awards in Hospital," *Arkansas Democrat-Gazette*, June 8, 1966.

"Cambrian Communications Named One of Nine 'Red Hot Start-ups' by America's Network," *Business Wire*, April 18, 2001.

Carroll County Bowlder, April 28, 1877, courtesy of Mary Etzbach Campbell.

"Clark Announcement Disturbing to Clinton," *Washington Post*, July 31, 1999.

Clark announcement speech as posted on Clark04.com.

"Clark Campaigns at Light Speed," *Wired*, September 30, 2003.

"Clark Challenges Kerry's, Others' Openness," *Nashua Telegraph* (New Hampshire), January 26, 2004.

"Clark Claims Oklahoma, and First Victory of Political Career," *New York Times*, February 4, 2003.

"Clark Derides Clinton Conspiracy Rumor," Associated Press, December 11, 2003.

"Clark Endorses Kerry's U.S. Presidential Campaign," Bloomberg.com, quote.bloomberg.com/apps/ news?pid=10000103&sid=acmoCfPBe7ts&refer=us

"Clark Named to Top Europe Post," DefenseLink, posted April 1, 1997, www.defenselink.mil/news/Apr1997/ n04011997_9704011.html.

"Clark Papers Talk Politics and War," *Washington Post*, February 7, 2004.

Clark remarks made at the Democratic National Committee Fall Meeting, October 3, 2003, www.genclark.com/policy/ wandp.htm.

"Clark Says Bye to Job at Stephens," *Arkansas Democrat-Gazette*, March 1, 2003.

"Clark Says He Would Have Voted for War," *New York Times*, September 19, 2003.

"Clark Set Sights on the Stars in Boyhood," *Atlanta Journal-Constitution*, December 7, 2003.

Clark speech excerpts as posted on the Annenberg Political Fact Check site, FactCheck.org, www.factcheck.org/ article.aspx?docID=97.

"Clark to Launch Media Blitz," *Washington Post*, November 16, 2003.

"Clark Under Sharp Attack in Democratic Debate," *Washington Post*, October 10, 2003.

"Clark Wants Civilian Reserve to Provide National Service," *New York Times*, October 15, 2003.

"Clark's Earnings Are Way Up," *Washington Post*, December 16, 2003.

Clinton speech, May 4, 1999.

CNBC/Wall Street Journal Presidential Debate, September 25, 2003, www.gwu.edu/~action/2004/primdeb/deb092503tra.html.

"Comment: Success of Military Diversity Proves Affirmative Action Works," *Detroit Free Press*, October 24, 2003.

"Daunting Intellect Sets Clark Apart, and Some People Off, in Soldier's Life Ringed by Success," *Associated Press*, October 30, 2003.

"Democrat Carrier Wins Allsopp Award," *Arkansas Democrat-Gazette*, December 22, 1965 (Clark presented award to new winner).

"Democrats Mix It Up in Debate," CNN.com, September 26, 2003.

"Digitization: Key to Landpower Dominance," *Army*, November 1993.

"Draft Clark 2004 for President Committee Files with FEC," US Newswire, June 18, 2003.

Electric Vehicles World.com, www.evworld.com/audio/wclark1.rm.

"Europe Salutes Allied Force Commander," American Forces Press Service, May 4, 2000.

"Field Notes: Wesley Clark," ABCNEWS.com, abcnews.go.com/sections/Politics/DailyNews/fieldclark.html.

"For Auto Executives, Greener Roads After Retirement," *New York Times*, October 2, 2003.

"Frontline," PBS interview with Wesley Clark, www.pbs.org/wgbh/pages/frontline/shows/kosovo/interviews/clark.html.

"Future Star," *Fortune*, September 15, 2003.

"Gen. Wesley Clark Resigns from Stephens," Arkansas Business.com, February 28, 2003.

"General Clark on the Hustings," *New York Times*, November 23, 2003.

"General Clark: Kosovo Belongs to All," United Press International, May 2, 2000, www.comtexnews.com.

"General Clark's Battles," *New Yorker*, November 17, 2003.

"General Relativity (Retired)," usnews.com, October 1, 2003.

"General Takes Helm of Motor Maker," *Automotive News*, April 28, 2003.

"A General's Life on the Outside," *U.S. News and World Report*, July 3, 2000.

"Hail to the Scribe," *Variety*, September 22, 2003.

"Hall Grad, Cadet, Gets Top Grades," *Arkansas Democrat Gazette*, August 4, 1964.

"A Hero to Some; To Others, Headstrong," *Washington Post*, October 19, 2003.

"His Family's Refugee Past Is Said to Inspire NATO's Commander," *New York Times*, May 3, 1999.

"History of Little Rock Public Schools Desegregation," www.centralhigh57.org/1957-58.htm.

"Home State Record: Wesley Clark," New Hampshire Public Radio News, www.nhpr.org/view_content/5529.

"How a Presidential Candidate and a Texas Doctor Share History, But Not Life," *Arkansas Democrat-Gazette*, November 16, 2003.

"How We Fight," *Time*, April 26, 1999.

"'I'm Spiritual. I'm Religious. I'm a Good Christian,'" Beliefnet.com, www.beliefnet.com/story/136/story_13636_1.html.

"In His Own Words," *Washington Post*, October 19, 2003.

"Inside Wesley Clark," *Arkansas Democrat-Gazette*, July 13, 2003.

"Intellect Helped Lead the Way," NWArkansasOnline.net, November 15, 2003, www.nwaonline.net/pdfarchive/2003/november/15/11-15-03%20A16.pdf.

"Is Wesley Clark a Democratic Ike or Bill's Clone?" *New York Observer*, October 15, 2003.

"A List of 67 Major Telecom Bankruptcies," *Converge Digest*, October 10, 2002, www.convergedigest.com/Mergers/financialarticle.asp?ID=4160.

MacArthur's speech before Congress, April 20, 1951, Great American Speeches Web site, www.pbs.org/greatspeeches/timeline/#1960.

"MacArthur's Speeches" on pbs.org, www.pbs.org/wgbh/amex/macarthur/filmmore/reference/primary/macspeech06.html

"Military Units Experiment with Ultralight Vehicles," *National Defense*, June 2003.

"NATO, Moscow Bicker Over KFOR Troops," *Moscow Times*, July 6, 1999.

"A New Democratic Dark Horse?" *Time*, November 25, 2002.

"On the Issues: Protecting the Environment," www.clark04.com/issues/environment.

"One Degree of Separation," *New York Times*, December 7, 2003.

"Optimist Club Hears Story of West Point," *Arkansas Democrat-Gazette*, December 29, 1965.

PC-radio.com streaming audio, www.pc-radio.com/clark-nasa.mp3.

"Politics Has to Stop at the Water's Edge," *Wall Street Journal*, September 26, 2003.

"Presideo Expands Board with Appointment of General Wesley Clark," Business Wire, January 31, 2001, www.findarticles.com/cf_dls/m0EIN/2001_Jan_31/69752197/print.jhtml.

"Q&A: The Power of Two," *Newsweek*, September 18, 2003,

"Race for the White House 2004: Clark Profits from Ties to Pentagon," *Wall Street Journal*, September 18, 2003.

"Ranking the War Pundits," *Esquire*, May 2003.

"Reflections on Europe," *Army*, June 2000.

"Road to the White House," *Pittsburgh Post-Gazette*, January 11, 2004.

"Soldier Reared in Little Rock Shot for the Stars, Collared 4," *Arkansas Democrat-Gazette*, April 14, 1997.

"Some Ex-colleagues Critical of Gen. Clark," *Argus Leader* (Sioux Falls), October 12, 2003.

"Special Message to the Congress on Urgent National Needs," May 25, 1961, John F. Kennedy Library and Museum Web site, www.cs.umb.edu/jfklibrary/j052561.htm.

"Spotlight On: Speakers Bureaus," *Public Relations Tactics*, May 2002.

"Thank You from Wes Clark," www.clark04.com.

"The General's New Battle," *People*, October 6, 2003.

"The Last Word," *Newsweek*, July 14, 2003.

"The Man for the Moment," *Newsweek*, April 5, 1999.

"The New Generation," *Arkansas Times*, January 25, 2002, www.arktimes.com/020125coverstorya.html.

"The Oldest Jewish Dynasty," Rav-SIG Online Journal, www.jewishgen.org/Rabbinic/journal/oldest.htm.

"The Record" Iowa Public Television transcript, January 12, 2004, www.iptv.org/iowapress/transcripts/2406.cfm.

"The Story of Billy Mitchell and the Little Rock Boys' Club," *Arkansas Democrat-Gazette*, February 28, 1954.

"The Unappreciated General," *Washington Post*, May 2, 2000.

"To Find Party, General Marched to His Own Drummer," *New York Times*, October 5, 2003.

"Virtual Politics," *The American Prospect*, October 2003.

"War Crimes Trial of Slobodan Milosevic and the Cross-Examination of General Wesley Clark," National Public Radio's "All Things Considered," December 16, 2003.

"War's Conduct Creates Tension Among Chiefs," *New York Times*, May 30, 1999.

"Washington Journal," C-Span, January 25, 2004.

"Washington Journal," C-Span, January 26, 2004.

"Washington Whispers," Free Republic.com, www.freerepublic.com/focus/f-news/830732/posts.

"WaveCrest Laboratories Names Former NATO Commander General Wesley K. Clark as Chairman," prnewswire.com/mnr/WaveCrestlabs/10740.

"We Want Answers: Wesley Clark," *Maxim*, November 2003.

"Wesley Clark in His Own Words," *Business Week*, November 24, 2003.

"Wesley Clark Is Fourth Democratic Candidate Touting His Jewish Connection," RealNews.com, www.realnews247.com/featured_story_wesley_clark's_jewish_connection.htm.

"Wesley Clark Named LRBC 'Boy of Year,'" *Arkansas Democrat-Gazette*, February 19, 1962.

"Wesley Clark Raises More than $3.5M in Fortnight," *Forbes*, October 6, 2003.

"Wesley Clark's Stepbrother Surprised to Learn of Family Tie," *New York Times*, November 16, 2003.

"Wesley K. Clark," *Boston Globe*, November 17, 2003.

"Wesley K. Clark," WashingtonPost.com, November 5, 2003.

"Wesley K. Clark: Candidate in the Making," *Boston Globe*, November 16, 2003.

"Wesley Kanne Clark," *Arkansas Democrat-Gazette*, November 30, 1997.

"West Point Cadet to Address Students," *Arkansas Democrat-Gazette*, March 15, 1964.

"West Point's No. 1 Honored, Lauds Arkansas's Progress," *Arkansas Democrat-Gazette*, August 3, 1966.

"What's in a Name? For Clark, Clues to His Jewish Heritage," *JTA*, www.jta.org/page_view_story.asp?intarticleid =13321&intcategoryid=3.

"White House Assigns Fellow to OMB Office," *Arkansas Democrat-Gazette*, June 29, 1975.

"White House Fellow Predicts War," *Arkansas Democrat-Gazette*, August 1, 1976.

"Who Is Aaron's Heir?" *New York Times*, January 19, 1997.

"Who Is Wesley Clark?" ABC News.com, www.abcnews.go.com/sections/WNT/Politics/Who_Is_Wesley_ Clark_040107.html.

"X-Ray Vision for G.I. Joe," *Business Week*, October 17, 2002.

BOOKS

Albright, Madeleine, *Madame Secretary* (New York: Hyperion, 2003)

Atkinson, Rick, *The Long Gray Line* (New York: Henry Holt, 1989)

Clark, Wesley, *Waging Modern War* (New York: Public Affairs, 2001)

——————, *Winning Modern Wars* (New York: Public Affairs, 2003)

Daalder, Ivo H., *Getting to Dayton* (Washington: Brookings Institution Press, 2000)

Ellis, Joseph, and Robert Moore, *School for Soldiers* (New York: Oxford, 1974)

Engeman, Jack, *West Point: The Life of a Cadet* (New York: Lothrop, Lee & Shepard, 1967)

Galloway, K. Bruce and Robert Bowie Johnson, Jr., *West Point: America's Power Fraternity* (New York: Simon & Schuster, 1973)

Grant, John, James Lynch, and Ronald Bailey, *West Point: The First 200 Years* (Guilford, CT: Globe Pequot Press, 2002)

Halberstam, David, *War in a Time of Peace: Bush, Clinton, and the Generals* (New York: Simon & Schuster, 2001)

Holbrooke, Richard, *To End a War* (New York: Random House, 1999)

Nelson, Jack, *Terror in the Night* (New York: Simon & Schuster, 1993)

Pizer, Vernon, *The United States Army* (New York: Frederick A. Praeger, 1967)

Priest, Dana, *The Mission* (New York: Norton, 2003)

Scales, Robert H., *Certain Victory: The U.S. Army in the Gulf War* (Dulles: Brassey's, 1994)

Truell, Peer, and Larry Gurwin, *False Profits: The Inside Story of BCCI, the World's Most Corrupt Financial Empire* (Boston: Houghton Mifflin, 1992)

Tucker, Spencer C., *The Encyclopedia of the Vietnam War* (New York: Oxford, 1998)

Tyrrell Jr., R. Emmett, *Boy Clinton: The Political Biography* (Washington: Regnery Publishing, 1996)

United States Military Academy 1962–1963 Catalogue, West Point, New York

University of Arkansas Little Rock Public History Seminar,
  *From the Ground Up: The First Seventy-Five Years at Joseph Pfeifer
  Kiwanis Camp* (Little Rock: Kiwanis Activities Board, 2003)
Volkman, Ernest, *A Legacy of Hate* (New York: Franklin Watts,
  1982)

INTERVIEWS

Allen Andersson
Mary Etzbach Campbell
Daniel Christman
Terence B. Clark
John E. Craig
Jim Dailey
Stewart Early
Jack Jacobs
Barry Kanne
Margaret Kolb
Jack LeCuyer
Wally Loveless
Tom McMahon

Phillip McMath
Mike Mehaffey
Boonie Miller
Charles Miller
Joseph Z. Perry
Harriet Salk
Diana Scales
Robert H. Scales
Gordon Suber
Sanford Tollette
Dale Vesser
Patty Loveless Watts
John "Jack" Wheeler

Military Records

All remarks from Clark's military records are from copies of
those records provided by the legal department of the
Clark04 campaign.

NOTES

★ ★ ★

PREFACE

[1] "Space History Milestone: Sputnik 1 Launch," Space.com, www.space.com/news/sputnik42_991005.html.

[2] Speech before Congress, April 20, 1951, Great American Speeches Web site, www.pbs.org/greatspeeches/timeline/#1960.

[3] "Clark Set Sights on the Stars in Boyhood," *Atlanta Journal-Constitution*, December 7, 2003.

[4] "Special Message to the Congress on Urgent National Needs," May 25, 1961, John F. Kennedy Library and Museum Web site, www.cs.umb.edu/jfklibrary/j052561.htm.

One: BEYOND THE PALE

[1] Author interview with Barry Kanne.

[2] Ibid.

[3] Kanne family records.

[4] Ibid.

[5] "Boy from Little Rock Chooses Military Path," *Boston Globe*, November 16, 2003.

[6] Ibid.

[7] Author interview with Mary Etzbach Campbell.

[8] "How a Presidential Candidate and a Texas Doctor Share History, But Not Life," *Arkansas Democrat-Gazette*, November 16, 2003.

[9] Ibid.

[10] Author interview with Barry Kanne.

[11] "Boy from Little Rock ..."

12 "'I'm Spiritual. I'm Religious. I'm a Good Christian,'" Beliefnet.com, www.beliefnet.com/story/136/ story_13636_1.html.

13 Ibid.

14 "Wesley Clark Is Fourth Democratic Candidate Touting His Jewish Connection," RealNews.com, www.realnews247.com/ featured_story_wesley_clark's_jewish_connection.htm.

15 "The Oldest Jewish Dynasty," Rav-SIG Online Journal, www.jewishgen.org/Rabbinic/journal/oldest.htm.

16 "Who Is Aaron's Heir?" *New York Times*, January 19, 1997.

17 Ibid.

18 "Boy from Little Rock ... "

19 "How a Presidential Candidate ... "

20 "Road to the White House," *Pittsburgh Post-Gazette*, January 11, 2004.

21 "His Family's Refugee Past Is Said to Inspire NATO's Commander," *New York Times*, May 3, 1999.

22 "A Hero to Some; To Others, Headstrong," *Washington Post*, October 19, 2003.

23 "Boy from Little Rock ... "

24 Author interview with Mary Etzbach Campbell.

25 Author interview with Barry Kanne.

26 *Terror in the Night*, by Jack Nelson, New York: Simon & Schuster, 1993, pp. 33–34.

27 *A Legacy of Hate*, by Ernest Volkman, New York: Franklin Watts, 1982, p. 32.

28 Nelson, p. 26.

29 Volkman, p. 148.

30 *Carroll County Bowlder*, April 28, 1877, courtesy of Mary Etzbach Campbell.

31 Author interview with Mary Etzbach Campbell.

32 Ibid.

33 How a Presidential Candidate ... "

Two: "BOY OF THE YEAR"

1 *New York Times*, March 6, 1966.

2 "'I'm Spiritual ... '"

3 "Who Is Wesley Clark?" ABC News.com, ww.abcnews.go.com/sections/WNT/Politics/Who_Is_Wesley_Clark_040107.html.

4 "Future Star," *Fortune*, September 15, 2003.

5 Author interview with Terence B. Clark.

6 "One Degree of Separation," *New York Times*, December 7, 2003.

7 Author interview with Terence B. Clark.

8 "One Degree of Separation."

9 "How a Presidential Candidate . . . "

10 "Boy from Little Rock . . . "

11 Author interview with Terence B. Clark.

12 "Wesley Clark's Stepbrother Surprised to Learn of Family Tie," *New York Times*, November 16, 2003.

13 "Who Is Wesley Clark?"

14 "The Record" Iowa Public Television transcript, January 12, 2004, www.iptv.org/iowapress/transcripts/2406.cfm.

15 "General Clark on the Hustings," *New York Times*, November 23, 2003.

16 "It's All Relative," *Fort Worth Star-Telegram*, November 17, 2003.

17 "Soldier Reared in Little Rock Shot for the Stars, Collared 4," *Arkansas Democrat-Gazette*, April 14, 1997.

18 Author interview with Wally Loveless.

19 Ibid.

20 Author interview with Mary Etzbach Campbell.

21 "Wesley K. Clark: Candidate in the Making," *Boston Globe*, November 16, 2003.

22 Author interview with Patty Loveless.

23 "Wesley Kanne Clark," *Arkansas Democrat-Gazette*, November 30, 1997.

24 *Washington Post*.

25 "How a Presidential Candidate . . . "

26 "A Hero to Some."

27 "'I'm Spiritual . . . '"

28 "The Story of Billy Mitchell and the Little Rock Boys' Club," *Arkansas Democrat-Gazette*, February 28, 1954.

29 "Wesley Kanne Clark."

30 Author interview with Boonie Miller.

31 "Washington Whispers," Free Republic.com, www.freerepublic.com/focus/f-news/830732/posts.

32 Author interview with Chuck Miller.

33 Ibid.

34 Author interview with Phillip McMath.

35 "Wesley Kanne Clark."

36 *Waging Modern War* by Wesley Clark, New York: Public Affairs, 2001, p. 21.

37 Ibid. (p. 21)

38 Ibid. (pp. 21–23)

39 Ibid. (p. 21)

40 *From the Ground Up: The First Seventy-Five Years at Joseph Pfeifer Kiwanis Camp* by the 2003 UALR Public History Seminar, Little Rock: Kiwanis Activities Board, 2003, p. 108.

41 "Wesley Kanne Clark."

42 "Democrat Carrier Wins Allsopp Award," *Arkansas Democrat-Gazette*, December 22, 1965 (Clark presented award to new winner).

43 "History of Little Rock Public Schools Desegregation," www.centralhigh57.org/1957-58.htm.

44 Author interview with Patty Loveless.

45 "History of Little Rock…"

46 Author interview with Patty Loveless.

47 Author interview with Phillip McMath.

48 "Boy from Little Rock … "

49 Author interview with Phillip McMath.

50 "Hall Grad, Cadet, Gets Top Grades," *Arkansas Democrat-Gazette*, August 4, 1964.

51 "Boy from Little Rock … "

52 "Comment: Success of Military Diversity Proves Affirmative Action Works," *Detroit Free Press*, October 24, 2003.

53 "Home State Record: Wesley Clark," New Hampshire Public Radio News, www.nhpr.org/view_content/5529.

54 Author interview with Phillip McMath.

55 How a Presidential Candidate … "

56 Arkansas Boys' State Web site, www.arklegion.homestead.com/Boys_State.html.

57 "Boys' Club Campers to Attend U.S. Academies," *Arkansas Democrat-Gazette*, June 20, 1962.

58 "Wesley Clark Named LRBC 'Boy of Year,'" *Arkansas Democrat-Gazette*, February 19, 1962.

59 "Wesley Kanne Clark."

60 "'I'm Spiritual ...'"

61 Author interview with Margaret Kolb.

62 Ibid.

63 Ibid.

64 Ibid.

65 *From the Ground Up*, p. 43.

Three: "THE CORPS, THE CORPS, AND THE CORPS"

1 "MacArthur's Speeches" on pbs.org, www.pbs.org/wgbh/amex/macarthur/filmmore/reference/primary/macspeech06.html.

2 "Wesley Kanne Clark," *Arkansas Democrat-Gazette*, November 30, 1997.

3 Ibid.

4 "Is Wesley Clark a Democratic Ike or Bill's Clone?" *New York Observer*, October 15, 2003.

5 "Wesley Kanne Clark."

6 All remarks from Clark's military records are from copies of those records provided by the legal department of the Clark04 campaign.

7 Author interview with Margaret Kolb.

8 "Battalion Commander," *Washington Post*, May 10, 1981.

9 "How a Presidential Candidate and a Texas Doctor Share History, But Not Life," *Arkansas Democrat-Gazette*, November 16, 2003.

10 *School for Soldiers* by Joseph Ellis and Robert Moore, New York: Oxford, 1974, p. 69.

11 "Boy from Little Rock Chooses Military Path," *Boston Globe*, November 16, 2003.

12 Ibid.

13 *West Point: America's Power Fraternity* by K. Bruce Galloway and Robert Bowie Johnson Jr., New York: Simon & Schuster, 1973, p. 67.

14 *United States Military Academy 1962–1963 Catalogue*, West Point, New York.

15 Author interview with John Wheeler.

16 Ibid.

17 "Battalion Commander."

18 "Wesley Kanne Clark."

19 Author interview with Jack LeCuyer.

20 Ibid.

21 "Boy from Little Rock . . ."

22 "Hall Grad, Cadet, Gets Top Grades," *Arkansas Democrat-Gazette*, August 4, 1964.

23 "Cadet Clark Gets Awards in Hospital," *Arkansas Democrat-Gazette*, June 8, 1966.

24 "Daunting Intellect Sets Clark Apart, and Some People Off, In Soldier's Life Ringed by Success," *San Diego Union-Tribune*, November 2, 2003.

25 Author interview with John Wheeler.

26 Author interview with Dale Vesser.

27 "Clark Campaign Defined by War Stance, Critics," *Sacramento Bee*, December 19, 2003.

28 *The Long Gray Line* by Rick Atkinson, New York: Holt, 1989, p. 30.

29 "MacArthur's Speeches" on pbs.org

30 "West Point Cadet to Address Students," *Arkansas Democrat-Gazette*, March 15, 1964.

31 "Optimist Club Hears Story of West Point," *Arkansas Democrat-Gazette*, December 29, 1965.

32 "Hall Grad . . . "

33 "Wesley Kanne Clark."

34 "The General's New Battle," *People*, October 6, 2003.

35 Ibid.

36 *The Long Gray Line*, p. 135.

Four: THE MILLION-DOLLAR WOUND

1 *The United States Army* by Vernon Pizer, New York: Frederick A. Praeger, 1967, p.173.

2 "West Point's No. 1 Honored, Lauds Arkansas's Progress," *Arkansas Democrat-Gazette*, August 3, 1966.

3 Author interview with Stewart Early.

4 Ibid.

5 Ibid.

6 "Boy from Little Rock ..."

7 *The Long Gray Line*, p. 228.

8 "Battalion Commander," *Washington Post*, May 10, 1981.

9 Author interview with Phillip McMath.

10 "General Clark on the Hustings," *New York Times*, November 23, 2003.

11 Author interview with Stewart Early.

12 "Boy from Little Rock ... "

13 "'I'm Spiritual.'"

14 Ibid.

15 Author interview with Stewart Early.

16 *The Long Gray Line*, p. 282.

17 Remarks made at the Democratic National Committee Fall Meeting, October 3, 2003, www.genclark.com/policy/wandp.htm.

18 "What's in a Name? For Clark, Clues to His Jewish Heritage," *JTA*, www.jta.org/page_view_story.asp?intarticleid =13321&intcategoryid=3.

19 "Wesley K. Clark: Candidate in the Making," *Boston Globe*, November 16, 2003.

20 "'I'm Spiritual.'"

21 Ibid.

22 "What's in a Name?"

23 All remarks from Clark's military records are from copies of those records provided by the legal department of the Clark04 campaign.

24 Author interview with Stewart Early.

25 "General Clark on the Hustings."

26 "General Clark's Battles," *New Yorker*, November 17, 2003.

27 *The Long Gray Line*, p. 155.

28 *Waging Modern War*, p. 23.

29 "We Want Answers: Wesley Clark," *Maxim*, November 2003.

30 Ibid.

31 Ibid.

[32] Transcript from the Presidential Candidates Forum on Women's Issues, November 5, 2003.

[33] "'I'm Spiritual.'"

[34] "Battalion Commander."

[35] "'I'm Spiritual.'"

[36] "Boy from Little Rock ... "

[37] "General Clark on the Hustings."

Five: IN COMMAND

[1] "Reflections on Europe," *Army*, June 2000.

[2] All remarks from Clark's military records are from copies of those records provided by the legal department of the Clark04 campaign.

[3] "Politics Has to Stop at the Water's Edge," speech given to the Pulaski Country Republican Party on May 11, 2001, as published in the *Wall Street Journal*, September 26, 2003.

[4] "Wesley Kanne Clark," *Arkansas Democrat-Gazette*, November 30, 1997.

[5] *Waging Modern War*, p. 17.

[6] *Certain Victory: The U.S. Army in the Gulf War* by Robert H. Scales, Dulles: Brassey's, 1994.

[7] Author interview with Jack Jacobs.

[8] Ibid.

[9] Author interview with Daniel Christman.

[10] Ibid.

[11] *Waging Modern War*, pp. 5–6.

[12] "How We Fight," *Time*, April 26, 1999.

[13] "White House Assigns Fellow to OMB Office," *Arkansas Democrat-Gazette*, June 29, 1975.

[14] "White House Fellow Predicts War," *Arkansas Democrat-Gazette*, August 1, 1976.

[15] "'I'm Spiritual. I'm Religious. I'm a Good Person,'" Beliefnet.com.

[16] "White House Fellow ... "

[17] Author interview with John "Jack" Wheeler.

[18] Ibid.

[19] Ibid.

[20] *The Long Gray Line*, p. 477.

21 *Waging Modern War*, p. 24.

22 *Waging Modern War*, p. 24-25.

23 *War in a Time of Peace: Bush, Clinton, and the Generals,* by David Halberstam, New York: Simon & Schuster, 2001, p. 432.

24 *Waging Modern War*, p. 25.

25 *War in a Time of Peace,* pp. 432–433.

26 Army Gen. Maxwell Thurman, Military.com, www.military. com/Content/MoreContent/1,12044,Mlthurman,00.html.

27 Author interview with Robert Scales.

28 Ibid.

29 Author interview with Diana Scales.

30 "Is Wesley Clark a Democratic Ike or Bill's Clone?" *New York Observer,* October 15, 2003.

31 "Inside Wesley Clark," *Arkansas Democrat-Gazette,* July 13, 2003.

32 Transcript of "Washington Journal," C-Span, January 25, 2004.

33 Ibid.

34 *War in a Time of Peace,* p. 433.

35 *Waging Modern War,* p. 25.

36 Author interview with Daniel Christman.

37 Ibid.

38 "Hail to the Scribe," *Variety,* September 22, 2003.

39 "Digitization: Key to Landpower Dominance," *Army,* November, 1993.

40 *Waging Modern War*, p. 26.

41 "An Arkansas Alliance, and High-ranking Foes," *Boston Globe,* November 17, 2003.

42 *Waging Modern War,* p. 26.

43 "Clark Derides Clinton Conspiracy Rumor," Associated Press, December 11, 2003.

44 *Waging Modern War,* pp. 26–27.

45 Author interview with Daniel Christman.

46 "Politics Has to Stop . . . "

47 *Waging Modern War*, p. 28.

48 *Waging Modern War,* p. 40.

49 *Waging Modern War,* p. 52.

50 *To End a War* by Richard Holbrooke, New York: Random House, 1999, p. 9.

[51] "Wesley K. Clark," *Boston Globe*, November 17, 2003.

[52] *To End a War*, pp. 10–13.

[53] *Waging Modern War*, p. 66.

[54] *Waging Modern War*, p. 56.

[55] "Reflections on Europe."

[56] "The Man for the Moment," *Newsweek*, April 5, 1999.

Six: FOUR STARS

[1] *War in a Time of Peace: Bush, Clinton, and the Generals*, New York: Simon & Schuster, 2001, p. 427.

[2] *Waging Modern War*, p. 68.

[3] Author interview with Robert Scales.

[4] Ibid.

[5] Author interview with John "Jack" Wheeler.

[6] Author interview with Allen Andersson.

[7] "General Clark's Battles," *New Yorker*, November 17, 2003.

[8] *Waging Modern War*, p. 68

[9] *Waging Modern War*, p. 69

[10] "Field Notes: Wesley Clark," ABCNEWS.com, abcnews.go.com/sections/Politics/DailyNews/fieldclark.html.

[11] "Politics Has to Stop at the Water's Edge," speech given to the Pulaski Country Republican Party on May 11, 2001, as published in the *Wall Street Journal*, September 26, 2003.

[12] "Wesley K. Clark," *Boston Globe*, November 17, 2003

[13] Ibid.

[14] "Clark Named to Top Europe Post," DefenseLink, posted April 1, 1997, www.defenselink.mil/news/Apr1997/n04011997_9704011.html.

[15] *Waging Modern War*, p. 78.

[16] Clinton speech, May 4, 1999.

[17] "Wesley K. Clark . . . "

[18] "Balkan Nights," *US. News and World Report*, April 5, 1999.

[19] *War in a Time of Peace*, p. 421.

[20] PBS "Frontline" interview with Wesley Clark, www.pbs.org/wgbh/pages/frontline/shows/kosovo/interviews/clark.html.

[21] *Madame Secretary* by Madeleine Albright, New York: Hyperion, 2003, p. 409.

[22] *War in a Time of Peace*, p. 457.

23 *Waging Modern War,* p. 342.

24 "War's Conduct Creates Tension Among Chiefs," *New York Times,* May 30, 1999.

25 *Waging Modern War,* p. 269.

26 *Waging Modern War,* p. 273.

27 *War in a Time of Peace,* pp. 477–478.

28 *War in a Time of Peace,* p. 478.

29 "Clark Papers Talk Politics and War," *Washington Post,* February 7, 2004.

30 "Confrontation Over Pristina Airport," BBC News, March 9, 2000, news.bbc.co.uk/2/hi/europe/671495.stm.

31 "NATO, Moscow Bicker Over KFOR Troops," *Moscow Times,* July 6, 1999.

32 *Waging Modern War,* p. 403.

33 *Waging Modern War,* p. 408.

34 *Waging Modern War,* p. 409.

35 *War in a Time of Peace,* pp. 478–479.

36 "Wes Not Ike," National Review online, August 21, 2003, www.nationalreview.com/comment/comment-dowd082103.asp.

37 *The Mission* by Dana Priest, New York: Norton, 2003, p. 274.

38 "The Unappreciated General," *Washington Post,* May 2, 2000.

39 McCain press release, July 28, 1999.

40 "Clark Announcement Disturbing to Clinton," *Washington Post,* July 31, 1999.

41 Author interview with Daniel Christman.

42 "Belgrade plot to kill NATO chiefs in Kosovo," *Times* (London), March 28, 2000.

43 "Europe Salutes Allied Force Commander," American Forces Press Service, May 4, 2000.

44 "War Crimes Trial of Slobodan Milosevic and the Cross-Examination of General Wesley Clark," National Public Radio's "All Things Considered," December 16, 2003.

45 News conference press release, Federal Document Clearing House transcript, December 17, 2003.

46 "General Clark: Kosovo Belongs to All," United Press International, May 2, 2000, www.comtexnews.com.

47 *Waging Modern War,* p. 415.

Seven: BOARDROOM WARRIOR

1 "General Clark on the Hustings: Complexity and Contradiction," *New York Times*, November 23, 2003.

2 Ibid.

3 "A General's Life on the Outside," *U.S. News and World Report*, July 3, 2000.

4 Ibid.

5 "After Retirement, Clark Has Forged a Lucrative Career," *New York Times*, November 10, 2003.

6 Ibid.

7 "After Retirement ... "

8 Ibid.

9 "The New Generation," *Arkansas Times*, January 25, 2002, www.arktimes.com/020125coverstorya.html

10 *False Profits: The Inside Story of BCCI, the World's Most Corrupt Financial Empire* by Peer Truell and Larry Gurwin, Boston: Houghton Mifflin, 1992, p. 428.

11 *Boy Clinton: The Political Biography* by R. Emmett Tyrrell Jr., Washington: Regnery Publishing, 1996, p. 105.

12 "Spotlight On: Speakers Bureaus," *Public Relations Tactics*, May 2002.

13 "Clark's Earnings Are Way Up," *Washington Post*, December 16, 2003.

14 "After the Army, Clark Signs Up as Businessman," *Arkansas Democrat-Gazette*, October 2, 2003.

15 Ibid.

16 "Race for the White House 2004: Clark Profits from Ties to Pentagon," *Wall Street Journal*, September 18, 2003.

17 "After Retirement ... "

18 "After the Army ... "

19 "Acxiom's Stake in Terror War Under Fire," *Arkansas Democrat-Gazette*, September 24, 2003.

20 Ibid.

21 "After the Army ... "

22 Author interview with Mary Etzbach Campbell.

23 "Race for the White House ... "

24 "X-Ray Vision for G.I. Joe," *Business Week*, October 17, 2002.

25 "After the Army ... "

26 "X-Ray Vision ... "
27 "Race for the White House ..."
28 "After Retirement ... "
29 "After the Army ... "
30 "America Must Be Prepared to Fight on a New Battlefield: The Cyber Front," Entrust Resources, www.entrust.com/resources/newsletter/dec02/article3.htm.
31 "Presideo Expands Board with Appointment of General Wesley Clark," Business Wire, January 31, 2001, www.find articles.com/cf_dls/m0EIN/2001_Jan_31/69752197/print.jhtml.
32 "After Retirement ... "
33 "Cambrian Communications Named One of Nine 'Red Hot Start-ups' by America's Network," *Business Wire*, April 18, 2001.
34 "A List of 67 Major Telecom Bankruptcies," *Converge Digest*, October 10, 2002, www.convergedigest.com/Mergers/financialarticle.asp?ID=4160.
35 "Are Old-time Telecoms Beyond Hope?" *Seattle Times*, October 28, 2002.
36 International Crisis Group Web site, www.crisisweb.org/home/index.cfm.
37 Atlantic Council Web site, www.acus.org/history.html.
38 "Permanent Alliance? NATO's Prague Summit and Beyond," posted in Atlantic Council publications archives, www.acus.org/Publications/policypapers/internationalsecurity/permanent%20Alliance.pdf.
39 Ibid.
40 "Gen. Wesley Clark Resigns from Stephens," Arkansas Business.com, February 28, 2003.
41 "Banker Runs off to Join the (Media) Circus," *New York Times*, March 9, 2003.
42 "Clark Says Bye to Job at Stephens," *Arkansas Democrat-Gazette*, March 1, 2003.
43 "Ranking the War Pundits," *Esquire*, May 2003.
44 "Clark Challenges Kerry's, Others' Openness," *Nashua Telegraph* (New Hampshire), January 26, 2004.
45 "After Retirement ... "
46 "After the Army ... "

47 Ibid.

48 Ibid.

49 Ibid.

50 "After Retirement . . . "

51 "Intellect Helped Lead the Way," NWArkansasOnline.net, November 15, 2003, www.nwaonline.net/ pdfarchive/2003/november/15/11-15-03%20A16.pdf.

52 Author interview with Tom McMahon.

Eight: GENERAL RELATIVITY

1 "Clark Campaigns at Light Speed," *Wired*, September 30, 2003.

2 "General Clark on the Hustings: Complexity and Contradiction," *New York Times*, November 23, 2003.

3 *Waging Modern War*, p. xx.

4 *Wired*.

5 "General Relativity (Retired)," usnews.com, October 1, 2003.

6 Author interview with Joseph Z. Perry.

7 Ibid.

8 Author interview with Allen Andersson.

9 "Bike Boffins Pedal with General Clark," *Moscow Times*, September 23, 2003.

10 www.evworld.com/audio/wclark1.rm.

11 Author interview with Joseph Z. Perry.

12 Ibid.

13 Ibid.

14 Ibid.

15 Author interview with Allen Andersson.

16 Author interview with Joseph Z. Perry.

17 Ibid.

18 Ibid.

19 "Military Units Experiment with Ultralight Vehicles," *National Defense*, June 2003.

20 "General Takes Helm of Motor Maker," *Automotive News*, April 28, 2003.

21 Author interview with Joseph Z. Perry.

22 "WaveCrest Laboratories Names Former NATO Commander General Wesley K. Clark as Chairman," prnewswire.com/mnr/WaveCrestlabs/10740.

23 "For Auto Executives, Greener Roads After Retirement," *New York Times*, October 2, 2003.

24 www.evworld.com/audio/wclark1.rm.

25 "Wesley Clark in His Own Words," *Business Week*, November 24, 2003.

26 "Transcript: Wesley K. Clark," WashingtonPost.com, November 5, 2003.

27 "On the Issues: Protecting the Environment," clark04.com/issues/environment.

28 *Wired.*

29 www.pc-radio.com/clark-nasa.mp3.

30 Author interview with Joseph Z. Perry.

Nine: "WELCOME TO THE PARTY"

1 "The Last Word," *Newsweek*, July 14, 2003.

2 Ibid.

3 "A New Democratic Dark Horse?" *Time*, November 25, 2002.

4 "We Want Answers: Wesley Clark," *Maxim*, November 2003.

5 "In His Own Words," *Washington Post*, October 19, 2003.

6 "To Find Party, General Marched to His Own Drummer," *New York Times*, October 5, 2003.

7 "Q&A: The Power of Two," *Newsweek*, September 18, 2003.

8 "Virtual Politics," *The American Prospect*, October 2003.

9 "Q&A..."

10 "Draft Clark 2004 for President Committee Files with FEC," US Newswire, June 18, 2003.

11 Author interview with Gordon Suber.

12 Ibid.

13 Gertrude Clark interview on C-Span's "American Journal," January 25, 2004.

14 "Draft Clark 2004 for President..."

15 Announcement speech as posted on Clark04.com.

16 "Wesley Clark Raises More than $3.5M in Fortnight," *Forbes*, October 6, 2003.

[17] "Clark to Launch Media Blitz," *Washington Post*, November 16, 2003.

[18] Author interview with Gordon Suber.

[19] Transcript of Democratic Primary debate, September 25, 2003, www.gwu.edu/~action/2004/primdeb/deb092503tra.html.

[20] "Clark Says He Would Have Voted for War," *New York Times*, September 19, 2003.

[21] "Clark Under Sharp Attack in Democratic Debate," *Washington Post*, October 10, 2003.

[22] "To Find Party . . . "

[23] Speech excerpts as posted on the Annenberg Political Fact Check site, FactCheck.org, www.factcheck.org/article.aspx?docID=97.

[24] "Democrats Mix It Up In Debate," CNN.com, September 26, 2003.

[25] "Some Ex-colleagues Critical of Gen. Clark," *Argus Leader* (Sioux Falls), October 12, 2003.

[26] "Clark Wants Civilian Reserve to Provide National Service," *New York Times*, October 15, 2003.

[27] Author interview with Mary Etzbach Campbell.

[28] Posted on Clark04.com

[29] "Material Girl Covers Clark with Praise, CNN.com, December 16, 2003, www.cnn.com/2003/ALLPOLITICS/12/16/elec04.prez.clark.madonna.

[30] "Thank You from Wes Clark," www.clark04.com.

[31] "Clark Endorses Kerry's U.S. Presidential Campaign, Bloomberg.com, quote.bloomberg.com/apps/news?pid=10000103&sid=acmoCfPBe7ts&refer=us.

[32] "Clark Claims Oklahoma, and First Victory of Political Career," *New York Times*, February 4, 2003.

[33] Author interview with Gordon Suber.

[34] Author interview with Wally Loveless.

[35] "Battalion Commander, *Washington Post Magazine*, May 10, 1981.

[36] CNN.com, www.cnn.com/2004/ALLPOLITICS/02/11/elec04.prez.main.

[37] Clark speech, December 1, 2003, clark04.com/speeches/014.

ACKNOWLEDGMENTS

✯ ✯ ✯ ✯

The greatest pleasure in exploring the life of General Clark has been in meeting a host of people whose lives have touched his, and who were kind enough to share their experiences with me. I am deeply grateful to Mary Etzbach Campbell, who fascinated me with stories about her childhood with Wesley Clark in Little Rock, including a private tour of Pulaski Heights. I will always remember her hospitality and generosity in sharing family records and photographs. I am also indebted to several others for their Little Rock insights: Phil McMath, Wally Loveless, Patty Loveless Watts, Margaret Kolb, Reverend Randy Hyde, Mayor Jim Dailey, and Charles Miller and his mother, Boonie. Sanford Tollette of the Joseph Pfeifer Kiwanis Camp has my admiration for the important, life-changing work he is doing and my thanks for an inspiring tour of the facility that played such an important role in Clark's life.

Many thanks go to Barry Kanne, a Clark family expert who never tired of talking about his cousin; his wonderful conversations and vital information helped make this book complete. Thanks also to Harriet Salk, another family historian, for talking to me about the Kanne family, and to Terence B. Clark for sharing his stories about the Clarks.

I am grateful to Allen Andersson, Joe Perry, Tom McMahon, and Mike Mehaffey for giving me invaluable glimpses into Clark's scientist persona. And my warm appreciation goes to Robert and Diana Scales, Stewart Early, Jack LeCuyer, John Wheeler, Jack Jacobs, Dale Vesser, and Dan Christman for sharing stories about their backgrounds with Clark, each of which contributed significantly to this book.

I am indebted to Mary Jacoby of the Clark campaign for her assistance in helping me obtain contacts and military records, to Gordon Suber for his insights on the Draft Clark movement and campaign, to John E. Craig for a fascinating tour of the National War College, and also to Barbara Layton for her gracious assistance at a wonderful gala evening in New York. Very special thanks go to Esther Margolis of Newmarket Press for bringing this wonderful project to me, and to my editors, Keith Hollaman and Shannon Berning, for their professionalism, enthusiasm, and support. Also, I am thankful for Paul Sugarman's design and production expertise and Devon Spaght's excellent research assistance.

And loving thanks to my husband, Stanford, for taking the time to read and comment, chapter by chapter, during his very busy schedule. His feedback was vital, as usual, and his encouragement and enthusiastic interest made all the difference.

INDEX

✯ ✯ ✯ ✯

ABOUT THE AUTHOR
★ ★ ★ ★

Antonia Felix is the author of fourteen nonfiction books including the biographies *Condi: The Condoleezza Rice Story*, also from Newmarket Press; *Laura: America's First Lady, First Mother*, which spent several weeks on the *New York Times* extended bestseller list; *Andrea Bocelli: A Celebration*; *Silent Soul: The Miracles and Mysteries of Audrey Santo*; *Christie Todd Whitman*; and *Wild About Harry: The Illustrated Biography of Harry Connick, Jr.*

Ms. Felix has appeared on CNN, CNN International, C-Span's *Booknotes*, *Entertainment Tonight*, *Inside Edition*, *Fox & Friends*, Pure Oxygen, *Judith Regan Tonight*, dozens of regional news programs, and over 100 radio programs. She has been profiled in the *Chicago Sun-Times*, the *St. Paul Pioneer Press*, and the *Corpus Christi Caller-Times*, and in 2003 she produced and hosted "The Writing Life," a television show about local authors in South Texas.

In addition to her writing career, Antonia is a classical singer who has sung in concerts and recitals throughout the United States and Europe, including Paris, Prague, and Moscow. She studied at the University of Wisconsin and the Mannes College of Music in New York, and received an M.A. in English from Texas A&M University. Ms. Felix lives with her husband near Kansas City.